'In a world where France has no word for E~~ntrepreneur~~
two: David Hall. You simply cannot read o~~ne at~~
a time, they are compelling, educational and very entertaining. ~~Names~~
have been changed to protect the guilty, and you will find yourself
laughing as you learn. David has shared one example for each of the
years he has been in business, and he knows that success only comes
when people act on their knowledge. Sadly, many don't, so to make sure
he's even included summaries and toolkits to help you on your journey.
Thank you for finally sharing your lifetime's work – if you had been born
earlier, I could have read it earlier, and that would have made a massive
difference to my own career.'

Thomas G Martin,
Chairman, Arco Ltd

'David delivered his Step Change programme to all 54 of our branch
directors and when the penny dropped the results were staggering with
improved sales and profitability. I hope our story in *Telling Tales* and the
Step Change Toolkit will inspire others to develop their business.'

David Kilburn,
Executive Chairman, MKM Building Supplies

'David's frank advice founded on a wealth of experience and sound
research has helped me grow my business 10-fold and provide sustained
shareholder value. He has also worked with my board to ensure alignment
and focus. This book will be invaluable for those entrepreneurs who want
to make a step change in their business performance.'

Martin Lauer,
Founder and MD, The One Point

'I have found David's experience to be invaluable in the support he has given me and the team. His *Telling Tales* principles provided invaluable guidance in developing and delivering our strategy whilst unlocking our potential as individuals and as a team. I am proud to say David is an adviser to our business and I regard him as a friend.'

Rob Daysley,
Owner and CEO, Designs

'David Hall knows about people. He knows about entrepreneurs and he knows about business. He is not another one of those who appear to have knowledge and expertise, he is authentic, and this come from decades of being immersed in this world and its characters. He knows also that we learn best through stories and that these build a folklore that creates a culture. Over the years I have heard David recount many tales from his vast experience and have always found them inspiring and informative. This has always left me wanting more, so I am delighted he has decided to commit his Tales to a book that I can visit and revisit. It is a cracking read.'

Paul Sewell,
Chairman, The Sewell Group

'Several years ago your advice and your Toolkits helped us grow from a small to a medium sized business c.50 people. Your Step change approach and candid input made attending your sessions a real joy. The mantras like 'Let go to Grow', 'Work ON the business' and 'Get the right people on the bus', enabled me to get the right mindset to grow my business. I am delighted to see you have included these ideas in your new book, which I will dip into from time to time to make sure I stay on track.'

Rob Brocklesby,
Owner, Brocklesby Ltd

'David's experience of business growth combined with the practical tools he offers business owners in *Telling Tales* is invaluable for any entrepreneur looking to grow their business.'

Sally Wray,
Owner, GoHire

'I've known David and his work for three decades. I've witnessed his commitment to empowering entrepreneurs and helping them build valuable businesses. David has a real skill in distilling complex issues into digestible forms and providing pathways to progress through his pragmatic approach. Business owners I'm sure will appreciate this insight into the techniques that David uses with clients. Maybe this collection of Tales will inspire others too.'

Dr Simon Haslam,
Chair of Academic Fellows, International Council of Management
Consultancy Institutes

'David is a source of invaluable, useful wisdom on how to run a successful business, having dedicated many years to helping businesses in a range of different sectors. He has a unique ability to get to the heart of a problem and turn his observations into practical advice that can transform a business's performance. My favourite piece of advice from David – the one that has served me consistently over the years – is "unplanned action beats planned inaction every time!"

Jane Molloy,
Director, Learning a Living Ltd

'David is truly a messiah for successful entrepreneurs. His ability to get to the core of the issue and provide apt solutions for his clients is simply amazing. The plethora of toolkits that David has refined over the years appear out from his magic box in a flurry and does the trick. His clarity and step by step approach brings workability in execution. David's knack of connecting the dots, strategizing and executing projects with aplomb, is truly his hallmark. I have seldom seen a consultant who thinks constantly of entrepreneurship success as he does. My best wishes to David for *Telling Tales* to be a reference guide to all entrepreneurs for fulfilment of their purpose.'

Jagadish Shenoy,
Executive Vice President, Edelweiss Financial Services Limited, Mumbai

'I have known David for 30 years. He was an eager disciple, keen to learn how to apply my models in his own work. We collaborated on several projects then he went onto use my processes and insights successfully in his own consulting practice.'

Gerard Egan,
Emeritus Professor of Organisational Development and Psychology,
Loyola University Chicago.

'David has helped the management team at Gordons on a number of occasions. He has a way of simplifying the issues and bringing clarity to the choices to be made. Plus, it was good fun dealing with him...'

Paul Ayre.
Managing Partner, Gordons LLP

'Delighted to see another brilliant publication from Prof David Hall. Although David has an academic title, truly deserved, he really is a 'pracademic'. David has not only created and sold a successful business but has been the adviser/counsel/mentor/trainer to hundreds of other businesses in his career, forty plus of the stories he shares in *Telling Tales*. This book is brimming with case studies: highlighting both the highs and lows of setting up and running a business and the learning that comes from this. Many stories and lessons learned are offered in this book, in an easy to read style, along with 10 DIY toolkits, to enable the reader to learn from their own experience and, importantly, how to put things into practice. David brings things to life with his 'tales' which enable the reader to understand how it might relate to them and importantly, how to take action. To me, this is the true value of the book. David is a management magician, Yoda for many of his clients. This is an essential book for anyone who wishes to grow their business successfully. Congratulations David on yet another truly insightful and practical offering.'

Dinah Bennett OBE.
Director, International Consultants for Entrepreneurship and Enterprise

'On a number of occasions The Outward Bound Trust had to square up to and resolve, some big issues. We found David's pragmatic and logical approach to problem solving immensely helpful. Funny, unsentimental and thorough – it was a blast of welcome realism. We went onto make good decisions with David's help that have stood the test of time.'

Nick Barret.
Chief Executive, The Outward Bound Trust

TELLING TALES

TELLING TALES

Lessons from a lifetime helping businesses succeed

David Hall

Management Books 2000

2000

First published in 2020 by Management Books 2000 Ltd
36 Western Road
Oxford OX1 4LG
Tel: 0044 (0) 1865 600738
Email: info@mb2000.com
Web: www.mb2000.com

British Library Cataloguing in Publication Data is available

ISBN 9781852527884

Contents

Dedication

Telling Tales is dedicated to the most important people in my life, my family:

Ellen
Simon
Darren
Natalie
Penny
Amelia
Maxwell
Sophie
Matilda
Jacob
Jude

Acknowledgements

My sincere thanks to Deb Henderson, whose help and advice in writing this book has been invaluable.

A huge thank you to my wife Ellen who helped me edit this book and kept my nose to the grindstone. I would not have finished the book without her encouragement and support.

A special thanks to the entrepreneurs who are the Rockstars of this book, for allowing me to share their tales for the benefit of others.

Finally thank you to Nicholas Dale-Harris for agreeing to publish our third book together and for your help and advice. Very much appreciated.

Chapter One
Introduction

Telling Tales is a compilation of the experiences of forty-four entrepreneurial leaders of SME businesses, with step by step toolkits to help you replicate their successes and avoid expensive mistakes.

Entrepreneurs are inspired by the tales of other entrepreneurs. They recognise aspects of themselves and their energy and self-belief are reignited. Inspiring others is the focus and purpose of this book – particularly relevant now as businesses struggle to recover from the Covid-19 nightmare.

These tales provide valuable lessons, told in the way that entrepreneurs prefer to learn – from those who have been there and done it.

Over more than four decades I have helped clients to develop their businesses, analysed what they do and shared this with others.

So, what do successful entrepreneurs do differently?

Typically, for example, they:

- create a **compelling vision** to provide focus and direction for their actions

- revitalise and reinvent their businesses using the **step change** process

- 'let go to grow' by delegating and focussing on removing the barriers to progress

- mobilise a **runner** to drive down costs
- engage in **partnering** by building mutually beneficial relationships with customers and suppliers
- actively use the **'working ON the business'** process to become much more effective
- **'get the right people on the bus'** – and the wrong people off it, quickly!

Regrettably, there will always be businesses who don't succeed. I have changed their names and details but have included their stories because they also provide valuable lessons – how not to do it!

Telling Tales consists of forty four Tales of business owners, who share their stories, warts and all.

There are 10 summary pieces, pulling together some of the key insights. Finally there are ten 'Toolkits', used by successful businesses to address their key challenges. The concept of the book is that the Tales create the inspiration and the Toolkits provide the process for you to create similar success.

Ready to go?

Right, let's crack on.

Chapter Two

Introducing David Hall

I was born in York in 1949 and effectively brought up by a single mum. Dad went into hospital when I was three years old and stayed there until I was 16. He suffered post-traumatic stress disorder having survived the carnage of Arnhem.

My younger brother Neville and I attended a Catholic school run by the De La Salle Brothers, where we were taught quite a bit about not masturbating (apparently God didn't like it), but very little on wrighting or rithmetic. Consequently, I left school with little expertise in either.

The Careers lady from the York Careers Service, Mrs Bainton, wore woollen tweeds and smelt of mothballs. She looked down her nose, sniffed me and pronounced,

'You're a big lad have you thought about the building industry?'

So obeying orders, I became an apprentice plumber. I hated it. I was useless at working with my hands. I counted down the minutes to home time, every day. I was so bloody hopeless that Brian Darley, my manager (and a really good guy) took pity on me and gave me a job in the office, as a trainee surveyor.

A kindly training officer, Raymond Elderton seemed to see something in me. Another good man. He sent me to Harley Street, London, for careers guidance. I completed several psychometric tests, and according to their careers expert their conclusion was: 'You should be a journalist, barrister or management consultant.'

I couldn't spell and didn't fancy wearing a wig, so I plumped for management consultancy, which sounded pretty good. I had no idea what it meant.

I stayed with the same organisation for another two years before moving to a training business which I hoped would be a first step towards management consultancy.

Over the next three years, whilst still employed, I read every business book I could get my hands on (my first wife described me as overdeveloped from the neck upwards); gained a Diploma in Management Studies, then a Master's in Management and spent evenings and weekends learning my trade, undertaking small consulting projects for local businesses.

Ten years on I decided I was ready to cut loose and set up my own consultancy practice. My boss Dr Frazer McVittie, suggested I continue to work for Steetley plc, two days a week and for myself the other three.

'It will give you a safety net for three years and reduce your risks.'

He was a kind, wise man. I owe him a lot.

On the 2nd June 1982 (the day the Falkland war commenced), I left the security of my 'proper' job and started my own management consultancy practice, hugely aware that I must make a success of my new venture, with three children to support and a mortgage to pay.

Before meeting our entrepreneurs, here are two short anecdotes about my early life which may have helped to shape me.

Chapter Three

Memories of an Altar Boy

'**God has called you.**' With these words, Father McAniff anoints me. I am an altar boy.

Wow! This could be my golden ticket to the Promised Land. I'm full of doubt, but not the strictly religious kind. Will I dong the bell on time? What if I spill the altar wine? Will my mates think I'm a wuz…?

Mum is so proud that I've been selected 'by God'. She always makes sure that my cassock and surplice are immaculate, patiently standing over the sink, rubbing away at the occasional red wine stain.

Father McAniff is a stern, rotund bull elephant of a man – I have never seen him smile. His breath smells of alcohol even before he glugs the communion wine at Mass. He has a jowly face, deep set eyes, a bald head and a forlorn expression.

'Dis is de turd Sundi of der mumf,' he proclaims from the pulpit, mangling the words in his thick Irish brogue. If one of the altar boys transgresses, he yells, 'Begorra – begone wit yer!'

During Mass, the heady smell of incense fills the church. Today is my turn – my first and last – to walk along the aisle, swinging the incense-burning vessel called the Thurible. Shakily, I overfill it, creating a dense fog in the church and leaving the congregation coughing and spluttering. I never get the job of Thurifer again. However, God works in mysterious ways and instead I'm allocated the job of pouring the holy wine into the chalice. Father Mcaniff is much less forgiving than my mum of the red spots on my surplice.

It is the 60's and St Allred's is a new modern building with clear glass windows, not the traditional stained-glass. The church is bright and airy, especially when the sun streams in. The sparse congregation are overall, elderly, dowdy and apparently devout. They shuffle slowly into the church, nodding at their friends.

The best bits for me are the hymns sung in Latin, which I grow to love: *Credo in unum Deum Patrem omnipotentem...* I love the poetry and ritual they bring to the Mass and, to me, they feel like the only meaningful connection with God in the whole service. (The Church decided to try to 'modernise' in the late 60's so the hymns were translated into English. A pity.)

The worst part of the service is the interminable sermon. Father Mcaniff must spend hours preparing them, yet he reads them verbatim from his notes without energy or passion. He may just as well be reading the railway timetable. A man going through the motions.

Finally the Mass is over, thanks be to God. The smattering of bored, fidgety children is shepherded out by their distracted parents faster than they came in. I watch from the altar as the rest of the congregation shambles out.

Even today, the smoky scent of extinguished altar candles lingers with me.

Chapter Four

Facing Fiery Fred
18th April 1966

It's my seventeenth birthday. It's the first day of my trial with Yorkshire County Cricket Club at their headquarters at Headingley in Leeds.

It has been quite a trek to get here. First, a number eleven bus to York railway station, a train to Leeds and then a bus from the station to the ground. I'm dressed for the whole journey in my Sunday best, (my only smart clothes) dragging my kitbag with me.

I arrived at the cricket ground early, but already some of the senior professionals are warming up at the nets. I immediately recognise the England players – Fred Trueman, Geoff Boycott, Ray Illingworth and Brian Close. I get changed hurriedly and join them, my heart thumping. I'm desperate to make a good first impression. There are five other young lads, from around Yorkshire, all keen to impress.

There are two netted tunnels, where batsmen practice their shots and the bowlers try to knock off their heads. There's no holding back – they're bowling at full pace, including a sprinkling of bouncers just to keep the batsmen on their toes.

'Boycott and Hall. Put your pads on,' orders the head coach, Ticker Mitchell. His real name is Arthur, but apparently, he got his nickname because of his habit of talking to himself whilst batting.

Boycott has hastily strapped on his pads and makes a dash for Net One. I soon realise why. Fred Trueman, infamous fast bowler for England, is bowling at full speed in Net Two. Boycott's no fool. Facing Fred in a match is bad enough, but in the nets he's a bloody nightmare – as I was about to find out.

It's not every day you face the world's number one fast bowler. It was an experience I will never, ever forget – but for more reasons than you might expect. I don't even see Fred's first ball, but I hear it whoosh past my head like a missile.

'What's up wi' thee, son?' barks Fred. 'Are you bloody blind?' He tucks his shirt back into his trouser waistband. He's surprisingly dishevelled and unkempt, as though he's wearing clothes three sizes too big, his long black hair trailing like the mane of a wild stallion.

I miss the next few balls. Then, somehow, I rock back and hit the next one out of the nets and it goes for miles. Fred pulls a stump out of the ground and storms down the pitch towards me, pointing it right at my face. He is so close that I could smell the beer on his breath. He was a like raging bull, spitting and snorting.

'Don't you fucking do that again, son!' he screams. 'The press is here to see me, not you, you little bastard!'

Ticker, hands on hips, joins in the tirade. 'You thought you'd hit a six, didn't you? Well you'd have been caught on the boundary. So, don't do it again, smart arse!'

During Fred's 'examination' of my batting technique, I noticed he was picking the seam of the cricket ball in his hand. I got an opportunity to examine that ball a bit later, whilst he was entertaining a small gaggle of reporters.

I was astonished. I noticed that he raised the seam of the ball at least quarter of an inch, by carefully rubbing it with the edge of a penny. No wonder he could make it jump off the pitch and whizz past your ear. Had I discovered Fred's secret?

Most of the players are dressed casually in old kit and jumpers – but not Geoff Boycott. He emerges from the dressing room immaculately turned out in his full England kit, complete with England cap, as if he's on a modelling assignment.

After he has batted, he returns to the pavilion without speaking a word to anyone. He gets changed and goes home. Everyone else joins in with the practice sessions, including the England stars. I don't think Boycott is a team player.

It's lunchtime. Ticker explains the 'rules' to the newcomers, including me.

'Right. The senior professionals go first to the buffet. You wait until they have got what they want, then it's your turn.'

There's not much left of the buffet when we get there. A few picked over cheese sandwiches, two sausage rolls and some crisps, to be shared out between six hungry young lads. Fred has piled his plate impressively high with enough food for the whole team.

Brian Close has brought with him two giant dogs, both about four feet tall. One wanders over to Fred's temporarily abandoned plate – he'd gone back to the buffet for more! – and starts wolfing down the mound of food. When Fred returns to his devastated plate, he goes berserk, screaming at the unrepentant dog and chasing it round the dressing room, cursing and trying to boot it up the backside. Us newbies try very hard not to laugh too loud.

Most of the England stars don't bother with us youngsters, although Doug Padgett and John Hampshire are a bit more approachable and offer me helpful tips on improving my batting technique. In fact, the stars barely speak to each other all day, either, which seems strange to me.

The day flies by and at the end Ticker comes over to me. 'Right, Hall. You did okay today, so see you next week. Here's your expenses.' He hands me a half crown. My best birthday present.

50 years on and looking back what did I learn from my time with Yorkshire Cricket?

I didn't take it seriously enough and never practised. I wish I had, as I would have loved to have been a professional cricketer. Professional sport has moved on light years. Fred used to have a couple of pints of beer before taking the field – no stretches and yoga for him in the warmup.

I'd like to think that I would have been more interested in young, hopeful players, had I become an England player, than those Yorkshire 'stars'.

Oh yes – and make sure you get to the buffet table quicker if you don't want to starve!

Chapter Five

Everyone needs a Gerry Egan

This is the story of my relationship with Gerard Egan, and why I became an 'Eganaut' (my phrase, not his).

It is 1987. I'm sitting on a plane to Chicago, looking out of the window at the billowing pure white cloud below us, musing on how I came to be making this journey.

Exactly a week earlier I had attended a lecture by a visiting American professor at York University. His name was Gerard Egan – I had never heard of him. In fact, I hadn't fancied going, but a friend persuaded me.

'David, this guy is a top man in the strategy field. You'll love him.'

I was up to date with most of the current business books, had attended several training programmes and recently gained a master's in management. I was enthusiastic and well prepared for my career as a management consultant, so I thought. I certainly had little appetite for yet another management workshop.

To say I was glad I went is an understatement. Gerard's charisma was irresistible. He shared his unique approach to business, together with his experiences as a management consultant. He had helped some of the world's largest businesses to succeed and it was obvious why they sought him out. He was truly mesmerising.

I thanked my friend, who had come with me to the lecture.

'See?' he said, looking at me triumphantly.

I've discovered a treasure trove of wisdom – and I'm going to grab with it with both hands. 'Yeah,' I said. 'He's brilliant!'

I approached Gerard Egan at the end of the lecture. We talked at length and got on well. We shared the same passion for helping businesses and for developing our understanding of the management role. Eventually I took a deep breath and said,

'Gerard, I would love to learn more about your way of working. How can I do that?'

'Okay,' he said, 'why don't you come and visit me in Chicago?' Wow! I wasn't expecting that.

I booked a flight to Chicago the following week. My wife thought I was crazy.

I'd had enough of the London underground, commuters crammed together like sardines in a tin, so I avoid the Chicago equivalent, nicknamed the 'L', and take a cab to Gerry's house. He'd told me to head for *The John Hancock*.

'This is *The John Hancock* sir,' the cabby announces as we pull up outside a massive high-rise building that seems to reach up into the clouds.

'Are you sure?' I enquire nervously, craning my neck.

'Yep. What's the address you got?'

'4440, *The John Hancock Building*.'

'Yep, that'll be the eighty-fifth floor.' I take the elevator. Gerry opens his door, greeting me with a big grin.

'Well, what do you think of my home?'

Nervously I approach the vast window. Way down below, North Michigan Avenue stretches away from us, streetlights glinting. It's known as the

Golden Mile, one of the prime Chicago real estate areas. It's breath-taking.

Gerry owns three condos on the eighty-fifth floor. I am allocated one all to myself, with wonderful views over Lake Michigan and Soldier Field, home of the Chicago Bears, the world famous football team.

'Gerry, the building seems to be swaying,' I say. 'Is it jet lag?'

He laughs. 'No, actually the tower is moving. Because of its height, it is designed to sway a metre in the wind, or else it might crack and fall down.' He's enjoying my mild discomfort, so he goes on, 'you might have noticed that the business offices are all below the sixteenth floor? That's because the directors discovered that if the wind blows the building over, it's designed to break and fall at floor twenty. So they should be left standing – or that's the theory!'

'That's great, Gerry,' I say sarcastically. 'So, we could end up in Lake Michigan?' Not sure how well I'd have slept that night without the jet lag...

I stayed with him several times after my first visit. Our friendship grew and I developed a deep understanding of his work. But I never quite got used to the swaying building.

The next day we get down to business and he begins to share his insights, methods and, best of all, his anecdotes, describing how he helped to train CEOs of some of the world's largest businesses. I feel like a kid in Willy Wonka's chocolate factory. Brilliant!

I discover that Gerry's family originally moved from Ireland to Chicago. There he studied as a Jesuit priest before leaving the Order a few years later. He qualified as a clinical psychologist at Loyola University in Chicago and stayed on to teach psychology. In 1974 he published The Skilled Helper, his seminal book, selling a million copies and now in its eleventh edition.

Whilst counselling CEOs on leadership, he realised that the major cause of stress and anxiety was the absence of structured management models.

Furthermore, because most managers were not trained to manage, their results failed to reach expectations. They were not equipped to take management seriously. He decided to try and help.

He developed processes and models that enabled CEOs to manage their businesses more successfully. For example, he identified that most businesses lacked a strategy process or business plan, consequently lurching from crisis to crisis – so he created a process that enabled managers to create a robust strategy. This provides focus and direction for everyone in the business.

He observed that those with a weak business culture inevitably performed inconsistently. He showed me how he enabled them to create their preferred culture; one that they wanted and needed to be successful.

'Managers need two vital sets of skills,' he told me. 'The first is managing people – recruiting, developing and guiding their performance. Secondly, they need processes to plan, solve problems and make decisions. Without these vital skills, they usually struggle.'

Gerry worked with American giants Amoco and Montgomery Ward, the World Health Organisation and businesses in Australia and the Far East. In the UK he has helped the BBC, BP, British Airways, the London Stock Exchange, Northern Foods, Selfridges and many more.

During my visits to Chicago, Gerry generously shared these experiences with me. I feel privileged that he felt enough confidence in me to share his techniques – I was one of a very small 'band of brothers'.

He said to me, 'Now we both have the tools and experiences to help solve business problems.' His enthusiasm is boundless and infectious.

I told Gerry a couple of my clients had said 'This is all common sense.'

He smiled and replied, 'Tell them we don't see too many clients with great management skills so maybe we should rename their comment as "rare sense".'

Since 1987 I have used his ideas and experiences to help dozens of clients to develop their businesses. Companies of all sizes, from ICI, Lafarge, Northern Foods, Weinberger, DB Schenker and Polypipe, to Keepmoat, MKM Building Supplies and local jewellers Hugh Rice. They have all benefited from Gerry Egan's methods.

He is a genius. He responded to the needs of largely untrained managers, creating a comprehensive system to help them take management seriously – and get results. He tutored me in his methods, enabling me in turn to help my clients tackle their own challenges. I shall be forever in his debt.

Reading this memoir, you might conclude that I love Gerry Egan. You are correct. I have used the methods he shared with me in my consulting practice for thirty-five years. I would never have got the same degree of insight from reading a book or attending a training course. This year Gerry turns 90 and continues to consult and share his wisdom.

Everyone needs a Gerry Egan. Go find yours.

Chapter Six

A love letter to Terry Bramall!

Part One

You **might find this** *memoir a bit long. But stick with it as it explains how I learned my craft in this organisation over 35 years. Many of the important things I learned in developing my career were learned with Keepmoat.*

In my forty years as a consultant I have worked with over ninety businesses. I would define three of these as truly great. Keepmoat is one of them. This is an account of how the owner of Keepmoat, Terry Bramall and I worked together to create a great business.

Gerry Egan gave me the tools. Terry Bramall provided the opportunity for me to learn how to apply them in his business.

In the early 1980s, when I first appeared on the scene, Terry's business had sales of £30 million and was haemorrhaging £250k of profits a year. In 2007, about twenty years later, the business sold for £783 million, a record figure for a privately-owned Yorkshire business.

Terry Bramall was born in Sprotbrough, South Yorkshire, in 1942, into the family construction business. Today, at seventy-seven, he is a slim, fit and handsome man, not a grey hair visible. This is a man determined to look after himself.

He told me, 'My aim is to live to be a hundred, so my approach to life is everything in moderation.' And that is how he lives: small meal portions, limited sugar and fat, the odd glass of wine, exercise, weight control, bed by ten, eight hours sleep at night…

But let's start at the beginning, I first met Terry in 1978 when I was learning the ropes as a consultant. He was considering buying ten acres of land on which to build seventy houses and I was brought in to research the local market. After spending time with estate agents, and the regional planning officer; it became clear to me that the 'opportunity' was a non-starter.

Boldly, I summarised my answer in a one word, one-page report. 'NO.'

'A thousand pounds for a "No"!' he hollered. Nevertheless, he paid my bill.

Little did we know, but this was the beginning of a brilliant, forty-year, mutually beneficial partnership. Twenty years later he confessed: 'That land in Thorne you looked at for me, remember? Well, it's still up for sale! It was a dud. If we had bought it, we'd have almost certainly have gone bust!' I think that was a thank you.

When the dust had settled on the sale of his business in 2007, we met up again. He was feeling nostalgic over the success of Keepmoat, so we reflected on the past forty years of its development, in preparation for a joint presentation of the Keepmoat story at a business conference in Hull.

'Do you remember, David, back in 1978, we were called Bramall Construction? Our first task was to get the business into profit.'

'Yep. That's when we reviewed your business strategy to find out where it was making and losing money. See *Toolkit 10: Redoing Your Strategy to Revitalise Your Business.* At that time you had made some rather random investments, the idea being to reduce risk by diversifying into a range of businesses. But as your only real interest was in construction, all the others were merely an expensive distraction. There was that outdoor pursuits training school in the Lake District, a window company and two squash clubs – remember?'

He grimaced. 'Don't remind me.'

'None of these eccentric "hobby businesses" as I would call them, ever made any profit, did they? And by my analysis were never likely to. The managing director of your hardwood window and door replacement business used a Guinness label as a tax disc in his company car – to save money, he said. Bonkers. Most of these businesses had issues and, if I remember rightly, in the end you didn't take much persuading to get rid of them.'

'We also had the joinery business,' Terry said. 'Chantry Furniture, making carved pews for churches. It lost 200k per annum. I kept hoping it would come good. You begged me to sell it.'

'And for three years you kept saying, "I think it'll turn around this year." Eventually, you told me why it meant so much to you.'

Terry smiled ruefully. 'It was where my dad started in business, fifty years ago. And, as you know, I still play the organ for my local church. It's one of my passions.' It had been an investment in nostalgia. With some reluctance on his part, we sold it.

Once we were liberated from Terry's smaller, distracting liabilities, we could focus wholeheartedly on his core activity, Bramall and Ogden.

When I had asked him to define the business, he said, 'We are a general contractor.' In practise this meant they would tender for any kind of building job, anywhere, for anyone, at any price. There was no strategy, so the net result was that sales were stagnant and profits non-existent.

Remembering this, Terry screwed up his face in agony. 'In those days, many general contractors tried to reduce risks by diversifying: they built schools, houses, hospitals and offices. Anything they could get their hands on. The aim was to have a full order book and keep staff in work. We didn't realise it at the time, but this approach dramatically increased the risks, ironically, because every job was a completely new experience for us. We had no track record.'

'A kind of "jack of all trades, master of none" – and your business was slowly going nowhere…'

Terry nodded. 'The moment of truth was at the board meeting when you said, "You guys are focussed on mediocrity." I was really taken aback. I stayed awake that night, thinking about it. You were right, we were mediocre. Things needed to change.'

'Yes and they did. We started with an historical, or as I said at the time, "hysterical" review of the past ten years' work. We needed to identify where money was made or lost, on different types of contracts. It became clear that refurbishing council houses which was where you consistently made profit.'

Terry said, 'Your analysis provided me with another game changing insight: we had been working hard to maintain jobs for our people and look after our customers, but we'd forgotten about the business owner. Everybody was happy – apart from me!'

Terry was a master of using setbacks to gird his loins and drive forward with renewed energy and spirit. Problems never did him in.

'Looking back in those days, it's hard to believe when I first joined the business my father didn't know how he was doing until the accountant's figures, six months after the year end,' Terry admitted sheepishly. 'So I put myself on a bookkeeping course to try and understand our finances.' He laughed. 'That was a waste of time! I hated the bloody course and gave up after three sessions. But I quickly got much better control of our numbers.'

Together we developed a new strategy for Bramall Construction based on our analysis of the strengths and weaknesses of the business, as well as the market opportunities and threats.

'It was the 80's. The Thatcher government was providing significant funds to local authorities to improve council houses in the eighties. This was a major opportunity for us. Our new mission statement was *to become the market leader in refurbishing council houses in the North of England*. And we did!' He recalled this change of fortune with a big grin.

'Another seminal moment, David, was when we recruited David Blunt as Finance Director.'

'Then there was a difficult one for you, as I remember, Terry. I informed you that the senior team was not strong enough and you were faced with some tricky decisions.'

So we reviewed the top team and, typically, Terry included himself in this process. He concluded that his role should be as investor rather than manager. So we decided to surround him with a team of people who had strong management skills, led by Dick Watson, his former Operations Director. Terry recognised that his strength was as a strategist, but Dick was someone who could be relied on to deliver the plan. This was a brave call on his part effectively relinquishing overall control of his business. I dubbed this *Letting Go to Grow* – see *Toolkit 9*. It turned out to be another positive game-changing decision.

I reminded him, 'In 1983 you bought another building firm, Frank Haslam Milan, which specialised in starter homes for local authorities. This enabled you to provide a full housing solution.' This was a shrewd acquisition. FHM complemented the existing Bramall business which focussed on regenerating existing council properties. But the newly merged businesses needed a revised plan, to capitalise on its new range of services.

'We couldn't choose between the two business names, Bramall's or FHM, for the new business, so we bought one off the shelf. We chose Keepmoat,' said Terry.

'That's when we conducted a customer perception survey to find out what our local authority customers really wanted. It became clear that they valued Keepmoat because you delivered projects on time and recognised that it was not just about building houses but, more importantly, about regenerating communities.'

'Yep, that was another real insight for us,' Terry said happily.

The survey also revealed that they 'delighted' their customers. See *Toolkit 5: Delighting Customers*. We trained their teams in the process, installing some culture-changing behaviours. In other words, we emphasised the importance of treating all clients' staff with respect; and we learned through experience to hire empathetic people, usually women, to deal with council tenants, rather than the 'hairy-arsed' builders on site.

As a direct result of these initiatives, local authorities began to receive positive feedback from their delighted tenants. Consequently, Keepmoat was, and remained, their preferred supplier. Happy days.

'Do you remember, Terry, how we nurtured the "customer delight" culture?'

'Remind me.'

'Every regional office audited the others to check that each was operating the new culture. After two years, this kind of audit was abandoned because, by then, the new culture had become embedded.'

'I do recall that our guys thought we were getting a bit corporate. But it worked.'

The morning had passed and now we were walking around his newly laid garden, sipping coffee to clear our heads. We agreed to meet again the following week.

Chapter Seven

A love letter to Terry Bramall!

Part Two

'Right, where were we?'
'2002, Terry. We'd got into partnering'.

'Ah yes. That was another stroke of luck for us. The government introduced a scheme called "partnering" into the building industry, creating mutually beneficial relationships between the client and the builder. Traditionally in the tendering for work process, builders had to put in low prices, often below cost, to win the work then had to work hard to make a profit. In partnering factors other than price such as quality, safety record and track record was considered.

'We had already been doing this for ten years via our "delighting customers" initiative, so we were ten years ahead of the competition.'

'Yes, and you capitalised on this competitive advantage for the next twenty years!' Terry smiled at me as if he were counting his winnings.

'Yes, so we changed the mission statement, based on customers' feedback, to *delivering community regeneration*. It wasn't just about building houses.'

Then more good fortune. In 2000, the Labour government, under Tony Blair, committed to a new initiative: investing billions to ensure that all council homes met their Decent Homes Standard by 2010. This meant regenerating thousands of homes across the UK. Keepmoat were in pole position to benefit from this windfall.

'Inspired by this new opportunity, we decided to become a billion pound business with £100 million profits. Sales, in 2000, were £100 million, so a billion was a really ambitious goal.'

'Yes, the initial reaction from management was sceptical: "Terry's off his head"; "it's a joke", "he must be crazy". In response, Terry, you donned your leadership hat and came to the rescue. You made a passionate announcement to your colleagues, I remember. "You are the best management team in the industry and I really believe if anyone can do it, you can." They were impressed.'

Terry said, 'One of the best things that you introduced, David, was our Keepmoat Academy. You established it to train and develop our managers. We hired the best consultants and trainers we could find, investing hundreds of thousands of pounds in developing management skills – the skills we required to make our business a success. It was money well spent.'

I added, 'We also developed a master's degree in management (MBA) for individuals identified as our future talent – the "hairy-arsed builders"! They were each assigned a coach and given projects working ON the business to broaden their experience and confidence. When opportunities emerged, the managers were trained and ready to go forward and grow the business.

'The aim was to create what Jim Collins, in his book, *Good to Great*, calls "Level Five Leaders". These leaders are great learners and develop their colleagues to enable them to produce results beyond expectations.

'We filled Keepmoat with Level Five Leaders everywhere – this was a critical ingredient in our success,' I recalled.

'Yes,' said Terry, 'at that time orders for new projects were exceeding expectations and sales were going through the roof. But so were costs and consequently profits were squeezed.'

'We needed to address that issue quickly,' I interrupted. 'We set up the "Ten Million Team", led by David Blunt. See *Toolkit 1: Working ON the Business*. Three commercial people, together with David and me, set about analysing opportunities to boost profits by ten million pounds. Our principle was simple: the easiest way to make money is to stop losing it. The next question we asked was, where is our biggest spend? Answer: seventy per cent went on buying materials and hiring subcontractors. Next question: how effectively do we buy? Analysis showed we were no worse than any other building contractor.

'Do you remember Terry? It was suggested, tongue in cheek, that we should hang a plaque on the wall, "*We are no worse than anybody else!*"'

'It was bloody true, unfortunately,' Terry replied with remembered frustration. It was unusual for him to swear.

I went on. 'We asked, so who *does* buy well? Answer: Walmart, the giant U.S. retailer who had recently purchased ASDA. So we asked the Walmart buyer to share their secret of buying success.'

The Keepmoat buying team was assembled and the Walmart buyer questioned them, listening patiently and occasionally shaking his head. 'That was how we operated, twenty years ago. Let me explain our buying policy now.' The Keepmoat team listened carefully, then adopted the Walmart approach, adding £90 million to company profits over the next ten years. Boom.

Over the next ten years we engaged in more than twenty-five profit improvement and efficiency initiatives. By working ON the business rather than simply IN it, we made significant improvements to Keepmoat's performance.

Result? Between 1997 to 2010, Keepmoat made ten per cent nett profits every year, whilst their competitors struggled to make four per cent.

This performance has yet to be repeated in the construction industry. Over thirteen years, Keepmoat worked hard and became a truly GREAT business.

In 2007, whilst the business was still riding the 'Decent Homes' wave of opportunity, Terry decided to retire. The business was sold for £783 million. Not a bad result.

When we had finished reminiscing over our thirty-five year working partnership, we stood up, looked at each other in the eyes for a few seconds and embraced for what seemed a long time. It was a lovely moment. Nothing needed to be said.

I hope that this story demonstrates how, by taking management seriously, it is possible to create a great business. Hard and challenging work, but well worth it.

Reflections on thirty-five years of working with Terry at Keepmoat

Most of all, it was the most mutually beneficial partnership I have ever experienced. Terry got what he wanted – a successful business, which he was proud to own. He gave me licence to experiment with new business concepts in his business. It was like having my own laboratory to experiment and try things. I learned so much from those experiences, knowledge which I have been able to share with many clients ever since.

What is Terry really like? First, he is a natural innovative leader. He has excellent interpersonal skills, he is charming, well-spoken and interested in people. This has been shown to be a key skill that many senior leaders possess – and he has it in spades. Terry is an easy person to like. He has a presence which you notice the minute he enters the room. He was always a good learner and he kept his ego in check – most of the time....

When we introduced a new programme, he would always volunteer himself to be on the first one because he was genuinely interested. This sent a powerful signal to everyone in the business. 'Terry's doing it, so it must be serious.' This is not the norm for owners and senior people in my experience.

He was always willing to delegate and trust people because we had made sure we got the right people on the bus.

He was prepared to invest and take calculated risks. Our best times were when we were speaking quietly together, as great friends do. In summary, Terry was a leader who people were inspired to follow.

We created a 'learning organisation' at Keepmoat, one that was never satisfied. It constantly searched for ways to improve its people and their performance. I believe this was the key to the company's success.

How did I help Terry?

Terry was very ambitious and quickly recognised he had very little experience or knowledge of best practice. He also did not want to spend the time that I'd invested in studying how to build a successful business, so he willingly used my expertise. He had an open mind and, unusually for CEOs, he was prepared to admit when he needed help.

He told me, 'You were always honest with me, David. You told me some uncomfortable truths and I came to value and trust your opinion. I needed someone I could respect to look me in the eye and be straight. You introduced the latest and most effective management practices into our business and helped us on our journey from good to great.'

What did I gain from partnering with Terry?

Terry invested heavily in the programmes and initiatives I proposed and was happy if he gained some success or learned something from them.

I have been able to take these experiences and case examples to other clients over the past thirty-five years, so the partnership with Keepmoat has undoubtedly helped me grow my consulting practice. Also, my links with the successful Keepmoat brand has provided real credibility in the eyes of other clients.

Being both an insider and an outsider, close to Terry and the business not too involved in company politics, I felt I could be brutally honest, without fear or favour. I had other clients as well as Terry, which I think removed some of the pressure. He once said to me,

'David, I can discuss business with you in a way I can't with anyone else. Your added value is your independence and your honesty.' I was aware other senior managers felt I had too much influence with Terry, but in a way, I quite liked that.

I have never worked with anyone quite like Terry or his business and don't think I ever will again. He treated me with real dignity and respect, trusted me and enabled me to grow and become a successful consultant. Working at Keepmoat never felt like going to work. It was always exciting, fun, dynamic – and bloody brilliant

Thank you, Terry George Bramall CBE.

Chapter 8

Keepmoat – my final chapter

When Keepmoat was sold in 2007, it was agreed that Terry Bramall and Dick Watson would leave the business, whilst David Blunt would remain and become CEO. This would ensure continuity for the new investors.

David Blunt had joined Keepmoat in 1980 as the management accountant. Born in Goldthorpe near Doncaster, David started life as a professional footballer, an attacking midfielder, with Chester FC. He trained and qualified as an accountant whilst still playing football.

As a boy, his father took him to the races. 'We sat on the grass – couldn't afford the stands. I loved it. I remember the punters after the races, sitting on the bus and throwing coins out of the windows to us kids, as they drove through Goldthorpe.' The passion for racing stayed with David. When he became successful at Keepmoat, he invested in buying his own racehorses.

Over the years, David and I had worked together, right up to the sale of the business. We built a strong partnership based on trust, complementing each other skills: David's commercial and financial acumen and my entrepreneurial approach to finding and facilitating solutions to business challenges.

Immediately after the sale, he offered me a deal to keep me on – a generous retainer and a long-term incentive plan, plus my own office in the directors' suite. I was given more authority and responsibility to make changes to the business to boost sales and profits and I relished it. Together with Dave Hughes, my internal resource partner, we scoured the business for new opportunities to improve performance. These were exciting times – like getting my own train set to play with!

Over the next five years, Dave Hughes and I initiated over 25 new projects. For example we significantly reduced costs in the new homes business, making houses more affordable and therefore enabling more people to buy a new starter home. We introduced 'lean manufacturing', the Japanese approach to improving efficiency which reduced our costs. We limited each subcontractor's ability to pass on their extra costs to us, which we could not reclaim from our local authority clients. See *Toolkit 4: Cut Costs & Increase Profits.*

Eventually, in 2012, the investors, Caird Capital, who had acquired the business from HBOS, decided to 'merge' Keepmoat with another business they owned called Apollo. The purpose was to create a larger business, reducing competition and increasing the value when they sold it on. Apollo's were based in the South of England with sales of £400m but their profits were 4%. Keepmoat's, whose heartland was the Midlands and North and had sales more than £700m with profits of 10% and were regarded as the exemplar in the industry.

We were told Keepmoat was acquiring Apollo. However the investors appointed the Apollo Chairman as the leader of the newly 'merged' businesses. It quickly became clear that Apollo was regarded as the lead business in this merger, a reverse takeover!

During this period things got tough for David Blunt. He was having to deal with ever-increasing demands from the new investors, whilst endeavouring to protect his management group from Caird Capital's thirst for detail. Board meetings were now dominated by investor language, covenants, EBITDA, and discounted cash flow. As a result, the culture of the Keepmoat business (once its biggest asset) was rapidly changing.

As the pressure for growth from the investors increased, the board took more risks, accepting projects outside the carefully constructed strategy. One significant digression, into the construction of retirement complexes, brought with it specific problems. 'Homes, but on a bigger scale,' it was argued, but the complexes required major mechanical engineering works, air conditioning, large scale kitchens and complex heating systems. These features lay well beyond Keepmoat's experience and expertise.

As things started to go wrong, so followed the inevitable financial losses. Several factors, I believe, combined to create this dramatic downturn in Keepmoat's fortunes.

Firstly, the investors' demand for ever increasing sales and profits led to more risky tenders for unfamiliar projects, away from the core strategy. Typically, venture capitalists expect to sell on the business in three to five years for a healthy profit. This requires a boost to sales and profits at almost any cost.

Secondly, the new regional manager of the loss-making part of the business proved to be incompetent and arrogant. Although not involved in his selection, I tried to help. I visited him, sat in his meetings, talked with his team, and was appalled at what I discovered. The Keepmoat culture had been abandoned and what was in its place was, frankly, cavalier, and chaotic.

I wrote a scathing report for the board and copied in the regional MD. He complained about me to his boss, saying I was interfering, and his boss agreed and told me to back off. I think by this time David was fighting too many fires with the investors. Sadly, three months later David left the business as we had worked brilliantly together. The company's reduced profit performance meant losses all round – including my hefty bonus.

I tried to work with the newly appointed Keepmoat CEO for six months, but it was clear we were never going to get on together. He was the exact opposite of the Keepmoat people I had loved working with for thirty-five years.

So, my time with Keepmoat was finished. I went into a kind of mourning for six months but then rediscovered the love for what I do with another client. But that story is for another day.

And I learnt an important lesson: if you find something wrong, don't back off, stick with it until it is sorted.

Chapter Nine
Socrates helps me out

I **gave a talk to** a bunch of budding entrepreneurs intent on starting their own new businesses. The event was organised by a Hull-based community interest company (CIC), For Entrepreneurs Only, set up with a group of successful local business people. We had two key altruistic motives: to help local business people to succeed, thus creating more jobs in the area. Twice yearly we run a course of six weekly workshops for around twenty aspiring people; these evening events are formulated and presented by the FEO team on a voluntary basis.

My contribution is to teach them some business skills and I call this session 'How to create a successful new business'.

They are a mixed bunch, young and old. Some have been made redundant, others have never had a job, others are younger, all aspire to run their own businesses. I don't want to lecture them and send them to sleep so I have decided to try my daughter Penny's approach to helping people learn. Penny is a highly competent secondary teacher. It's called the Socratic method, based on the work of the philosopher Socrates and involves asking questions rather than lecturing – a style which I will find challenging!

I asked Penny why she uses this approach in her teaching.

'Well at university I found that knowledge passes from the lecturer's notes to the student's book, and quite often through the mind of neither! That's not useful learning, other than for passing an exam, perhaps, if you have a good memory. With this method the teacher asks questions and waits for the students to suggest an answer, so they do the thinking, not the teacher.'

So I decide to try the Socratic method on my eager audience.

'How many of you have run a business before?' No hands go up.

'How many of you want to be successful?' Stupid question. I need to work on my introduction.

'In your current or past employment, how many of you have found and solved a customer problem?' Two hands go up, one near the front. I peer at the name badge.

'Right Joe, come up and tell us about it.'

Joe speaks confidently. 'I worked for a building company on site and was shocked by how much material was broken or damaged due to poor storage and handling. Then I investigated storage methods at builders' merchants. They use racks very effectively. So my business idea is to sell purpose-made racking to builders. I can demonstrate how it will save them money by reducing waste and make them more efficient.' He grins and looks at me.

'Great stuff, Joe.' I turn to the audience. 'So, what do we learn from Joe's story?'

A young woman calls out. 'He worked for a company and saw they had a problem he thinks he can solve.'

'Exactly. Many successful businesses are started by people who spot an opportunity whilst working for someone else. They find potential customers, suppliers and contacts that they can use in their new business venture.'

Right, next step.

'How many of you have all the resources – money, people and systems – that you need to start your business?'

A young man in the back row slowly raises his hand. 'Not me. How can we possibly afford all the stuff we need?'

'You can't unless you are loaded. Entrepreneurs start their business on a shoestring….'

Shit. I'm in danger of lecturing again... Back to Socrates.

'Okay. If you don't have the resources you need, how can you start a business?'

A young man with spiky gelled hair and wearing a brightly coloured Hawaiian shirt jumps to his feet. 'Well I would get people to help me. My mum would do the admin and a friend said she would deliver stuff for me, if I helped her with her IT stuff.'

Another guy chimed in. 'My mate said I could store materials in his shed.'

'Right, that's the idea. Entrepreneurs find ways of getting things done on the cheap by begging, borrowing and befriending people, as well roughing it at the start.'

'What about finding customers?'

'Do I need a website?'

I look around the room. 'What do other people think?' (Reckon I'm getting the hang of this Socratic stuff now.)

A smart middle-aged woman with orange hair says, 'I can't afford one right now. Not sure my customers would buy off a website. Do I need a brochure? A business card?'

The questions are coming thick and fast. This is great.

'Okay. To gain customers in the most cost-effective manner, you need to engage in sign- poster networking. Let me explain. In every sector there are well-respected people who know lots of other people. The trick is to find them and build a relationship – and their trust. They can introduce you to potential customers, with the bonus of their blessing.'

'Sounds bloody hard,' says the guy in the Hawaiian shirt.

'You're right, but this is a most cost-effective form of networking to grow a business. The only cost is your time.'

Yes, I know I'm lecturing again – but these are fledging businesses they don't know what they don't know. However, they are keen and there's a buzz in the room. The next half hour flies by.

'Who in FEO can help me with my business plan?' asks the lady with bright orange hair.

'Good question. Give me your details at the end and I will put you in touch with the right FEO person.'

An older man asks, 'Where can I find out more about this stuff?'

I smile modestly. 'Well, I wrote a book thirty years ago called *The Hallmarks for Successful Business*. It's still selling well. It became a BBC television series called 'Winning', which was awarded a BAFTA in 1992.' Enough of blowing my own trumpet...

I wind up the session. Hope they enjoyed it.

Later, keen to know how well I had used the Socratic questioning technique, I talk it through with Penny.

'Well, it sounds like you got them involved. But you need to ask *open* rather than *leading* questions and be prepared to wait and listen. Let them think for themselves a bit more. That's not easy I know for you, Dad. You do like the sound of your own voice.' I punch her arm lightly and she laughs. 'How did you feel it went?'

'It felt a bit clunky at first, but it did seem to engage them, perhaps more than my usual way of working. I'll try the Socratic method with my growth business sessions next. Thanks, Penny.'

'Okay, Dad. Crack on!'

Chapter Ten

Panic at Pertamina

It was 1983. My consulting practice was a year old and we were just getting going. A call came, out of the blue, from a client in London – we had completed a project together the previous year.

'David, do you fancy a project in Indonesia?'

'Erm, yes – but where exactly is that?'

'Southeast Asia. The client is called Pertamina, it's the state oil company of Indonesia. They want you to run workshops for them, over ten days, in best personnel practice.'

Cautiously I said, 'I'm flattered to be asked, but personnel practice isn't really my field of expertise.'

'Don't worry David – you'll know much more than they do.'

At that point I should have turned the offer down as I could embarrass myself and the client with my lack of experience, but I was young, keen, naive and needed the work. I said yes and, a few days later, signed the contract.

On my way to Heathrow Airport, I got another call from the London client.

'Pertamina have just confirmed that your fee will be £1000 per week plus expenses. Is that okay?'

I gulped. My usual fee rate in 1983 was £500 per day. But it was too late to back out. I felt stitched up – and things were about to get worse.

There were only around a dozen people on the Garuda flight from Heathrow to the Indonesian capital, Jakarta. A fellow passenger explained the empty seats. Garuda, the Indonesian state airline, currently had the worst safety record in the world….

When we arrived at Jakarta airport, I was greeted by an Indonesian gentleman who introduced himself as an agent for the project. He explained that he was working for another agent who had organised the project via another agent – my client in the UK.

So all these agents were a taking a cut of the fee and that's why my bloody pittance was so miserly... Happy days. It couldn't get any worse, could it…?

It did. Most of the thirty candidates on the programme spoke very little English. I had no Indonesian, of course. I spent the next ten days spinning out my limited expertise in personnel practice, all of us attempting to communicate in sign language and broken English. They were genuinely nice people and I felt like a fraud, letting them down. I think they were sorry for me and my situation.

I was staying in the government-owned Hotel Indonesia. It smelt mostly of the strong cigarettes that many Indonesians seemed to smoke. The manager, who happened to be English, offered to take me out to a brothel. I politely declined.

I was given a driver who chauffeured me around in a smart black Mercedes. I was not permitted to drive in Jakarta, which was a relief because the traffic was crazy, a weaving mass of cars, buses and motorcycles. Apparently, there are no rules about driving in the city. I kept my eyes shut all the time.

On the last day I recalled J. F. Kennedy's famous Berlin speech: *Ich bin ein Berliner.* Keen to ingratiate myself, I ended my farewell address with the equivalent phrase in Indonesian: *Saya Indonesian.* This left my audience in raptures. At last I had done something right.

I had been counting down the days to my flight home, so I breathed a sigh of relief as we entered Jakarta airport, glad that it was all over. But there was a sting in the tail. I was stopped going through customs. The security guard, wearing a gun, looked at my paperwork and said,

'Your visa has run out. You are an alien in my country. You cannot leave.'

Oh, fuck! He called another guard over, who pointed his rifle in my face.

'You cannot leave!'

Fortunately, in Departures I had teamed up with another Brit who was clearly more experienced than me.

'Offer him fifty dollars, quick!' he called across the security barrier. He had already gone through, so I was on my own.

I pulled out a note and the guard snarled, 'Okay. Go, go! Don't do it again.' He prodded his rifle right up my nose before letting me pass.

My heart beat like a train. I was sweating and panting for breath as I scurried away in search of the boarding gate.

Once on the plane, I bought several small bottles of gin and shared them with the guy who had saved me. Fortunately, I had also brought a clean pair of pants.

Since that time, some thirty-seven years ago, I am always anxious whilst waiting in a foreign airport for my return flight.

What did I learn from this horrible experience?

To take more control of projects at the start; avoid layers of agents and don't be romanced into taking on work if you can't do it justice, whatever the reward; to agree the fee up front, as part of the contract; and, importantly, research your audience. On a practical level, always check your visa details – and finally, fly with a reputable airline.

I learnt a lot from this.

Chapter Eleven

Leaders: the fabulous and the fatuous

You see it in the playground and on the sports field. Individuals who have the natural gift to organise and motivate their friends and their team members. But do you believe that they are born with management and leadership ability or can it be taught? What's it like to work for a great manager or if you are unfortunate enough – a poor one?

I am reading an interesting article entitled 'People leave their managers, not their companies.' The author suggests that between sixty and seventy five percent of people are disengaged at work, it's just a job, not a responsibility. Some leave because of poor management; or worse still in a way, many stay put, contributing little to their company.

This got me thinking of my own employment experience and reminded me of two particularly memorable managers, each for very different reasons. The first, let's call him Air Vice Marshall Jack Le Grundy (he was retired RAF top brass – how we won the war, God only knows). He could not remember my name and kept calling me John.

When it came to my annual appraisal, I was ambitious and looking forward to discussing my future. The AVM as he preferred to be called, cancelled the meeting three times, always at the last minute. I never got to discuss my career with him. He told me he had urgent business: his secretary divulged he was playing golf.

On one occasion we arrived at the front office door at the same time, I opened the door for him bowed and said, ironically, I hope, 'I know my place sir: it's to open doors.'

He replied, 'And I know mine John: it's to walk through them.'

He once accidentally dropped his pay slip on my office floor. I could not believe the salary he was on, particularly as most people, including me, thought he was useless. I pinned it to the company notice board for all to see.

I understand he got the job because of his connections with the right people in government, who could be helpful to our business. It certainly wasn't because of his management and leadership abilities.

Fortunately, my next boss, Tony Jones, was the exact opposite.

Annual appraisal time arrived. I entered Tony's office. He instructed his secretary to hold all calls and to bring a large pot of tea for us. He took off his suit jacket and settles into a comfy chair right next to mine. He leant forward looked me straight in the eyes, with a smile and said, 'Right David, I have been thinking about your career with us. I can tell you that the board are delighted with your work and we want to develop you.'

I struggled to control my excitement, nearly wetting myself.

'I have been looking at management courses for you', he went on, 'and we would like you to consider doing a Master's Degree in Management which of course we will pay for.'

It did not matter that being so close, I realise he had very bad halitosis.

Tony would ring me at night 'David we have a board meeting tomorrow can I run some ideas past you.'

My wife would complain 'Why is he ringing you at night?'

'No, no. he wants my advice.'

I would write papers for the board for him, with his name on, he would take his name off and put mine on.

If Tony rang me today, forty years later, and said 'David can you help me with a meeting in London tomorrow?' I swear my response would be 'Tony I will jump on a train right now.'

What do followers want from their leaders?

A recent study suggests three things:

- HONESTY – *tell me the truth even if it's bad news*
- INSPIRATION – *give me a reason to give my best for this business*
- COMPETENCE – *the skills to do the job*

How many leaders do you know who would score highly on these behaviours?

See Toolkit 8: Lessons from Entrepreneurial Leaders.

Now I reflect on the paper I have just read: *People leave managers not companies.* It's not rocket science to just show genuine interest in people and if you do, they will do almost anything for you. Treat them disrespectfully and they will just do the minimum.

I recall research I read years ago, that being 'interpersonally skilled', in other words the ability to communicate with people effectively, is a key skill effective manager possess. Tony had this skill in spades. I was not the only fortunate employee who really benefitted from his leadership qualities. Several of my colleagues also went on to develop successful careers with Tony's guidance and support.

If you want to get the best from your people, then here are a few things to try:

- *Be honest with people*
- *Listen carefully to what they say*
- *Ask questions rather than make statements*

- *Put your arm round people when they need it*
- *Take a genuine interest in them*
- *Treat them with dignity and respect*
- *Help them to achieve their dreams.*

Chapter Twelve

A happy dog's life at the Triple A Ranch

I **met Ann Adlington and** Arthur her husband, at their Triple A Ranch Animal Hotel for the first time in the 80's. This turns out to be an 'interesting' experience. Ann greets me with a big hug and a sloppy kiss. As I desperately try to disentangle myself from her clutches, I notice over my shoulder, a six-foot-tall oil painting of Ann and Arthur standing together.

I am here to discover how Ann can charge twice the rate for her business as her competitors and still have a full order book for the next twelve months. I start by asking Ann to explain the recipe for her amazing success.

'I was a critical care nurse At the Royal Victoria Infirmary in Newcastle, providing top quality care to seriously ill patients.

'We were going on holiday and I wanted to leave our dogs somewhere they would be happy, and I would be guilt free. I visited several dog kennels and was appalled at the standard of care offered. They were austere places with bare concrete floors. The animals were contained in small cages and most smelt strongly of urine or disinfectant. I could hardly bare to leave my dogs in those appalling conditions, so I persuaded a friend to look after them.

'When we came back from holiday, I decided to start my own dog kennels to look after people's dogs, to the same standards as I was used to as a nurse, caring for people.'

'How did you get started, Ann?'

'I'd heard about a national convention for dog kennel owners in California and decided to visit to get some inspiration. It was bloody amazing! Hundreds of exhibitors offering some crazy things for dogs: aerobics, swimming lessons, yoga and even singing lessons. It was mind blowing.'

'Then what, you had no experience at all.'

'That was a bonus. I was not limited by the conventional way of operating a dog kennel business, thank God. I had a blank canvas and so I designed my business based on my nursing experience; the visits to poorly run kennels and my experiences at the convention in America.

'We give each dog a personal carer, responsible the whole time it stays with us. We recruit young people who genuinely love dogs and are prepared to give them that extra bit of loving care. We make sure the pets are well fed, groomed, and exercised every day. I set up a course in dog welfare at our local college, for my staff, which gave them a Diploma in Dog Care. We set out not only to improve our people but to raise the standards in our industry. We must have done a good job because my people were constantly headhunted by the competition.'

Not sure Ann had any real competition her business was unique.

But that's not the full story. Ann explains that the kennels are kept scrupulously clean, more like a hotel than a dog kennel, which gave her the idea of calling it an animal hotel. In the marketing jargon, the pet ranch was repositioned for a more expensive market.

At the top end, one hundred and fifty pounds a week, pays for dog a dog bed, settee and dedicated companionship from someone who loves dogs. The regular customers come from far and wide, over a hundred miles in some cases.

I also discover that dogs can have up to four walks a day with the option of the agility course – the dog equivalent of an outward-bound circuit. Optional extras include aerobics, swimming, and hairdressing.

Dog owners feeling anxious about leaving their pet, can call Triple A and get a report on their dog's wellbeing, including a detailed description of their dog's stools!

Ann tells me 'When owners come to collect their pets, they usually have to drag them out of their "hotel room" and away from their new best friend, their carer.'

But what tickled me most is the cute idea of Ann sending post cards to their owners' home. When they get back from holiday, there is a card from Fido: 'I had a wonderful time, when can I go to the Triple A Ranch again!'

It's clear to me now how Ann can charge twice the price of her competition. It a completely different and an original proposition that delivers peace of mind for people who really care about their pets. Price is irrelevant to them. Ann delights her customers both dogs and owners. See *Toolkit 5: Delighting Customers.*

There are some important lessons for other businesses from Ann's story. If you give people something worth paying for, they will gladly pay you for it. Finally, nothing needs to be the same offer as every other business i.e. a commodity. You can add value to any product (even dog kennels) with fresh thinking. Ann disrupted the industry by learning from the latest best practice in the USA and her experiences as a nurse looking after people and applying it to the world of dogs. Boom!

Before leaving the Triple A, I was able to offer Ann some ideas to enable her to improve her profits. For example creating a system of Friends of Triple A, to encourage customers to commit to an annual membership to ensure their dogs could get a place when they needed it. I also suggested that dog clubs who meet regularly could use her facilities. It's possible to add value to any business, even a good one.

Ann is a pioneer who transformed the way dogs are treated when they owners are away.

Well done Ann. You deserve to succeed.

Postscripts:

1. Triple A won several national awards for innovative customer service.

2. Ann sold The Triple A Ranch to a multinational business who wanted to franchise it nationally. They cut out most of Ann's innovations to reduce costs. Sadly, it became a bog-standard kennel business and failed. Shame.

3. Ann now runs a successful fishing lake operation and a livery yard in Washington county Durham.

Chapter Thirteen
Mr Michael's Madhouse

Not every consulting job I have ever done has been a raging success – like most people, I have had my share of disappointments. One is permanently etched on my brain! It was the time I spent with Mr Michael.

Mr Michael had a clothing business in West Yorkshire. When I took on the project with him his business was in deep trouble. I was naive enough to think I could sort it for him. I was young, keen and needed to pay my mortgage.

'Hall, my personal assistant thinks I need help to sort a few little problems. I disagree I don't need this management stuff, but she tells me you're a good egg and I should give you a try.'

Mr Michael (he insisted on this title) was dapper but dated, his pinstripe suit shiny from wear. 'Old School', he was very posh, Harrow educated.

He introduced me to his son, Mr Charles who was on the payroll, but apparently, he only turned up to trouser the proceeds of the petty cash tin and fill his sports car, at the free company petrol pump.

I had only been there two hours and I was beginning to get bad vibes about this project, but ever the optimist, I told myself things can only get better.

I was introduced to Mr Henry, Mr Michaels Eighty-six-year-old elder brother and Financial Director. He also wore a suit which had seen better days and he looked like he desperately needed a shave and a shower. I asked him what the cash position with the bank looked like. He looked around vaguely, glasses on the end of his nose and replied,

'Ahem err good I think'.

Beam me up Scotty…

A week later I went back to Mr Michael's Madhouse. I was struggling to find anybody within the business I could trust to help me to identify the underlying problems so I could develop some solutions. However one thing was clear, they needed to get control of costs, or this business was going down the tubes.

The place was about to go bust. I discussed this with Mr Michael. 'We could ban all expenditure and give the staff a 10% pay cut,' he suggested.

'I agree with banning expenditure,' I said, 'but we should look for options other than cutting staff wages.'

'No time, Hall, no time to waste,' he blustered.

The pay cut was quickly announced to the 150 unhappy staff by a junior manager, not by Mr Michael he was playing golf. The very next day, he turned up, grinning in his brand-new powder blue Rolls Royce.

Unbelievable.

You could not make it up.

Very soon after the Rolls Royce incident Mr Michael offered me an opportunity to buy into his Lloyds of London syndicate.

'Hall I would like to invite you to join my syndicate, it's a real opportunity for you to get very rich.'

I was stupid enough to feel privileged to be asked.

For once fate was on my side, on the day I was due to visit him and sign up, it snowed heavily, and I couldn't make the meeting.

I later discovered that the syndicate was all over the news; it was about to go bust and its members, were trying to offload their losses onto naïve suckers like me. It was Mr Michaels syndicate.

The bastard.

The moral is if something looks too good to be true, it probably is. Thank God for the snow, or I could have been bankrupt. This was the final straw, I resigned from the project.

What did I learn from this experience?

Trust your instincts, the signs were there from day one: Mr Michael's attitude towards me and the project; Mr Charles appalling behaviour was sanctioned, Mr Henry the FD, who had no idea about the numbers, and finally the absence of any real talent in the whole place.

Some projects are not doable or desirable and this was one of them.

Chapter Fourteen

The Evolution of MKM Building Supplies

David Kilburn's **MKM Building Supplies** is an extraordinary tale of business success and provides inspiration to others seeking to build a successful business from virtually nothing. As consultant to David's business over ten years, I have helped him develop his business and witnessed its success at first hand.

David became an entrepreneur at the ripe old age of fifty. Before that he had worked for Harcros, a large corporate business where he 'served his apprenticeship', learning the ropes at somebody else's expense. Over twenty years he has worked to create the largest and most successful privately owned building supplies business in the UK.

I ask him about the old days and the challenge of working for Harcros.

He explains, 'Like most businesses in the sector we had strong central controls and lots of rules; we bombarded the stores with information, it was overload. It was very bureaucratic and demoralising for the people in the field, who were trying their best to serve the customers.'

'Was it frustrating for you personally?' I ask.

'Yes of course, but the good part was that I made some great contacts with customers, suppliers and key people in the industry. This was invaluable when I started out on my own.'

In a review of Harcros by Bain Consultancy in 1995, with its brief to reduce costs and improve efficiency, David was one of the casualties. Made redundant from a large corporate business, he had little option but to start out on his own.

'Who would take me on at fifty years old? I had no money. I was also separating from my first wife at that time.

'My new partner and I moved into a small flat, loaned to us by a friend. We had no furniture other than a small sofa and a tiny television. My friend's son turned up on Christmas Eve and commandeered the TV. We ate our first Christmas dinner together on our laps.'

He felt strongly that the Harcros approach was *not* the way to run a successful building supplies business. 'So when we started MKM I decided to do the exact opposite of the Harcros model.'

David's recipe for success is to compete on customer service, not on price; to poach existing branch directors in smaller towns, who bring with them their best staff and customers; to give these new directors a stake in the business; and to ensure that the centre serves the branches and limit central controls and bureaucracy.

So how was I involved in the development of MKM?

In 2010 I worked with David to design a new five-year strategy for the business, focussed on growth. It also helped identify the business priorities they needed to focus on to mobilise the strategy.

Between 2013 and 2017 I ran Step Change programmes for all MKM branch directors, a series of six intensive half-day workshops* providing business development tools to help them improve the performance of their branches. In the classic MKM way, branch directors were not told what to do but were given the help and support to create their own initiatives. They were provided with the Step Change Toolkit to enable them to put the lessons into practice and at every meeting they each reported on the impact and their resulting successes. See *Toolkit 2: Step Change.*

The MKM financial control system clearly showed how they each performed in terms of changes to their sales and profits.

David Kilburn's verdict?

'The workshops really helped transform the performance of a number of our branches. It gave the guys the tools to manage their branches more effectively. I was particularly pleased when, given that customer service is a number one priority, each of our branches came out top in every customer survey, reaffirming our strategy. This has been a very successful programme.'

Inevitably, not everything David tried has been successful. Take for example his attempt to recruit a 'clone' to manage his rapidly expanding business, he failed three times. The new recruits did not understand the unique MKM culture, each tried to impose his own management style, David knew it would hinder the company's success. He spotted the dilemma quickly enough to limit the damage.

Encouraged by new investors, Bain Capital, David is still seeking to recruit a fellow CEO. The irony is not lost on him that it was Bain's early efficiency consultation that lost him his job twenty five years ago. They are now more than happy to invest in him.

What is it about David that enabled him to start again at 50 years old and create the top business in the industry?

Firstly, he had been learning his trade for thirty years, making all the contacts he needed to start his business. Secondly, redundancy triggered his drive to succeed and desire to prove both Harcros and Bain wrong.

Finally, he has an almost perfect score on my Entrepreneurial Potential Report. This identifies whether people possess the skills and abilities needed to succeed as an entrepreneur. The report showed that David had all the skills required to be a successful entrepreneur.

MKM has grown faster than any competitor and makes higher profits. It has been voted Best Independent Builders' Merchant in the UK for five out of the past seven years.

In 2017 Bain Capital invested in MKM to fund its rapid growth plans. That year, sales hit £334 million. In 2020 they employ over 1650 people in over sixty branches nationwide.

What does the future hold for MKM? Will Bain, the new corporate investor, introduce a more formal structure and central controls? Or will they allow MKM to maintain its unique and highly successful culture and ways of working? How will David react if he feels the business is in danger of losing its DNA?

Whatever the outcome, the evolution of MKM under David Kilburn's leadership has been a remarkable success story.

The workshops include for example: Customer perception surveys to identify opportunities to improve their customers experiences. Using key dashboard information to improve sales and profits. Providing Leadership. Building a high-performance culture. Team-working. Letting go to Grow. Improving margins by reducing discounting.

Chapter Fifteen

Don't judge a book by the cover

Early in my career, when I was young, keen and naïve, I get a call, out of the blue, from Sir Norman Milton-Smyth's PA, Magenta.

'Sir Norman would like you to help him with his business.'

I am on the train to London the following day to meet the Great Man (I assume he must be great, with a name like Sir Norman ...)

I catch a bus to his Mayfair office. Magenta, a very smart, elderly lady with a hairstyle like Mrs Thatcher's, greets me rather sniffly, looking down her nose.

'Sir Norman has been held up at an important meeting. He should be available within the hour. You can wait over there.'

Two hours later the great man arrives, rather unsteady, reeking of alcohol. In his sixties, he is ruddy faced and dressed in a once expensive, but now rather shabby pin-striped suit.

'Hall! You have been recommended to me by a friend. I called because I need a bit of help with my business.' He farted loudly and then continued without missing a beat. 'We are in the construction business and were doing very nicely, but recently we seem to have lost our way. I am too busy, and I thought a fresh pair of eyes might help. Can you have a quick look at us and let me know what you think old boy?' He farted again.

I agree to spend a couple of days speaking to his people and reviewing his strategy and operations.

This exercise doesn't start well.

'Oh, so old Norm has hired you, has he?' His young Operations Director says with a smirk. This is rude and unprofessional, given we have just met and he doesn't know who I am.

I interview several of Sir Norman's team. I ask about the business strategy, focus, operation, systems and how they control the business. I also ask, tactfully, about Sir Norman's role as leader. He Is apparently well liked and respected by most of his team.

I decide not to write a report, but to present my findings to Sir Norman, face to face.

He appears at the agreed meeting time. He decides he needs to impress me.

'Did I tell you, Mr Hall, that I was a Colonel in Two Para – a paratroop regiment, you know. That's where I learned to lead men. And it's where I got this bloody limp. Shrapnel. War wound.'

I am stunned by this piece of personal information. I think for a moment and say,

'Actually, my father was also in Two Para during the Second World War. He was captured at Arnhem and, as a result, spent the rest of his life in and out of mental hospitals.'

Sir Norman's mouth drops, and he leans forward in his chair.

'Bloody hell, Hall! Your father was a war hero!' He pauses before asking, 'Did he know Colonel Frost, by any chance?'

I smile. 'Yes, he did. He was Dad's boss. Colonel Frost won the Victoria Cross for the Arnhem campaign.'

The atmosphere in the room has immediately changed. For over an hour we talk about Two Para, how they became the S.A.S. and the disaster at Arnhem.

Eventually we get around to discussing his business. Having listened to his business concerns and challenges for a couple of hours, in which he was very frank, I present my initial thoughts.

'Clearly this has been a successful business that has lost its way a bit. There seems to be no shared strategy or clear direction. You appear to be making the same mistake as many construction companies, by building anything, for anyone, at any time. A jack of all trades…'

He coughs, nearly choking. I'm on a roll, so I continue.

'Consequently you make money on some projects but blow it on others. The net effect is a loss.'

At that point he looks sheepish, but he's taking notes, which is normally a positive sign.

He asks, 'What do you suggest?'

'Well, you seem to be good at building new sites for McGinty and other food retailers, consistently making money on these projects. I understand that's because you negotiate, rather than compete on price with every other builder.'

He stands up and walks slowly to the window, gazing out on the park as I go on.

'I would seriously think about concentrating on these types of clients, it's obviously a growing a market.'

'Yes, but my guys like the challenge of building a variety of things.'

'It's a common problem in the construction industry, Sir Norman, so don't feel too bad about it. I have another construction client who, when facing the same problem, says to his people, "look if you want to gamble in the casino, play with your money, not mine!"'

'Mm, I get that. Anything else I ought to know?' he asks rather meekly.

'This might be a bit difficult, but I would also question whether your Finance Director is up to it. Your financial controls are poor, he should already have been asking these same questions about your strategy.'

He looks even more sheepish.

'Sir Norman, this is the "quick and dirty" assessment that you requested. I would suggest you get your team to explore these issues further.'

I put my documents into in my case and wait.

Sir Norman smiles at me. 'That's been very helpful David. Thank you. My friend, Terry Bramall, said you were a good egg – and he was right.'

I shrug, a little embarrassed. 'Terry has been a good client of mine, for over thirty years.'

On the train back home I reflect on my encounters with Sir Norman. I Initially thought he was posh and, frankly, arrogant: one of the 'born to rule' brigade. He was certainly from the other side of the tracks from me. However, he turned out to be a warm, friendly guy, just wanting his business to succeed and needing a bit of help – and not too proud to ask.

Memo to self: don't judge a book by its cover.

Postscripts

1. He paid my bill the day after I submitted the invoice. Very unusual. He called me and thanked me. He informed he had recruited a new finance man and had decided to follow my advice and concentrate on the markets they knew best.

2. Sir Norman and I exchanged personal Christmas cards for the next four years, when he updated me on the progress of the business. Then, one December, his cards stopped. Eventually I discovered that he had passed away. Another character gone.

Chapter Sixteen

Living the dream – the birth of DHP

When I started my management consulting practice in 1982, I was thirty-two, ambitious, full of hope, but frankly bloody naïve.

For the next five years I worked alone helping business clients to survive, change and grow. It was a great learning experience. I really enjoyed it.

By 1987 I was getting more projects which required experiences I did not possess, quality management, operations management and complex financial stuff for example. So I decided to hire people with the skills that were required.

I set up a business, David Hall Partnership Limited (DHP), to manage the growth we were enjoying. I was too naïve to recognise the risk in putting my home up as collateral with a bank to fund the business's growth. What could go wrong, never crossed my mind….

The phrase 'Partnership' was selected to describe how we wanted to work with clients and our colleagues in the business. I arranged for our colleagues to have business cards with 'Partner' on. My fellow directors did not approve, arguing it was naïve on my part. But the young trainees in our administration team thought it was brilliant, handing them out with pride, to their friends in the local pubs. It increased the engagement we got from them.

In the 1980's the Manpower Services Commission (MSC) later followed in the early 1990's by the Training and Enterprise Councils(TECs) and Business Links were set up by the Government to fund and provide training to people who were starting new businesses. We decided to take the 'Queen's shilling' and provide training under these schemes. DHP grew rapidly opening ten offices across the North of England and Scotland, employing 120 people.

I didn't enjoy the government funded business start-up, side of the business. It was frankly boring, but it was very profitable. I would be helping a corporate client during the day, then driving fifty miles in the evening to run a seminar for people starting businesses.

I became disillusioned, some people attended our programmes just to get their £25 per week on the Enterprise Allowance Scheme. I felt I was wasting my time and frankly theirs.

At this point DHP had two strands to it, the consulting business with private sector clients and the very lucrative public sector funded, business start-ups. I eventually delegated the running of this explosion in work with business start-ups to my colleagues who enjoyed the work.

In 1992 and 1994 I took sabbaticals from DHP and worked with the BBC on two 'Winning' business series. During this break from the business, I realised I was not interested in the business start-up work and I wanted to focus on my consulting work with private sector clients.

I had allowed my business to become over reliant on government-funded training which was a major distraction for the consulting arm I was most interested in.

So I decided to sell the start-up part of DHP in 1994.

This turned out to be a stressful process for several reasons.

Calling the business 'David Hall Partnership' turned out to be a big mistake. I wanted to leave the business, but it had my name on it. This proved a major hurdle in trying to sell it to a third party. So I was locked into a business that psychologically I had left.

Then the start-up business began to come under pressure from a reduction in government funding. Would I have anything to sell or would it go bust costing 120 jobs on my watch?

I considered other options for an exit and one was a management buyout. Fortunately one of my partners, who loved the start-up work, expressed an interest in leading a management buyout.

This partner and I had grown apart over the past years and I was nervous about doing a deal with him. At my suggestion we got an independent accountancy practice to put a value on DHP and agreed whatever value they came up with, we would use as the price.

The benefits were if we had got into disagreement over the price the only winners would be lawyers and accountants.

This plan worked, and it was one of the best decisions I made.

My partners asked me to stay on as Non-Exec Chairman. After some thought I declined, because with no shares or real influence, if it was raging success how would I feel or equally if it failed how would I feel?

It was a very difficult time because it felt like another divorce. I had given birth to DHP and now I walk away.

Once I had left the management buyout team started acquiring other businesses in the start-up market. This strategy succeeded for a while, but the government increasingly withdrew funding. In the end it was sold to another business.

The DHP era for me lasted from 1987 to the sale in 1995.

I went back to undertaking consulting projects for private sector clients which I am still doing today in 2020.

So what did I learn from my DHP experience?

The good stuff:

DHP helped over 10,000 people start a business over eight years.

I liked being an entrepreneur.

We invested in several colleagues to help them with their careers. Several have gone on to build international careers.

We always tried to do the right thing by colleagues and clients.

The bad stuff:

The financial adviser who I trusted with my pension and investments turned out to be a crook.

I tried to run a business that I was not interested in and this was stressful.

I invested in government funded projects that had a limited life span.

Risking my house as a loan guarantee with the bank was a naïve and stupid idea.

Chapter Seventeen

A visit to the Oracle

I **visited Oracle for the** first time in 2009. I caught a train to Reading, then the Oracle bus to their UK HQ just outside the town. This area is now known as the UK's Silicon Valley.

Oracle is a multibillion-dollar American tech giant, in the same league as Amazon and Twitter. The biggest business I have worked with, so I am apprehensive. What can I possibly offer them?

When I arrive, I am greeted by a young techie wearing jeans and a T-shirt. I notice they all wear jeans and T-shirt. I feel over-dressed in my suit.

'Mr Hall, welcome to Oracle. I'm Jasmine and I have arranged your induction, to get you up to speed with what we do. Cool.'

Jasmine shows me a video charting Oracle's amazing growth since 1977. Started by American Larry Ellison and two friends, Oracle dominates the business software market worldwide with sales in 2019 of over $39 billion US dollars. Over 95% of global corporate businesses use Oracle software. This is total market domination; no wonder Larry is always smiling. This guy is a true entrepreneur.

Wow. What am I doing here? A no tech Yorkshire lad with little experience of working with massive global businesses. I feel way out of my comfort zone. Maybe they have got the wrong David Hall?

Jasmine introduces me to the project manager, David Rajan. He is wearing faded jeans, David Bowie T-shirt and goatee beard. He explains,

'We dominate business software sales in large corporates worldwide. We now want to get into the midsized entrepreneurial business market, but we need help. We want to put on workshops for entrepreneurs across the UK, which we would like you to lead with your Entrecode research. Then we'll present our offer as part of these events. Cool, eh?'

I unbutton my collar and take off my tie.

'Cool, sounds like a plan.' (Christ, I'm using Oracle speak already.)

'We want you to deliver your Entrecode material, David. We particularly like your unique take on creating superior opportunities by identifying customer problems and then selling the solutions to the world. We love that and so will our clients.

'When you have warmed them up, we will then show them how we can help them to deliver the stuff you talk about using our software.'

'Okay,' I say, 'do you want me to include my research on how entrepreneurs think and act; are driven, persistent, have a positive attitude and are action oriented?'

'Yes, yes,' David says enthusiastically, 'our customers will love all that, it's why we hired you.'

Christ, I am thinking I should have doubled my fee rate.

David tells me the plan is to deliver twelve workshops across the UK in selected cities at smart venues primarily in the south of England.

First up is White Hart Lane, home to Tottenham Football Club, followed by St Albans and then Wembley.

The project lasts for six weeks, with one or two events a week, with forty to fifty medium sized businesses attending each event.

My presentation seems to be well received.

When the project is complete David tells me, 'We are delighted with the initial positive responses David, that we got from the attendees. You got rave reviews. We will follow up the new sales opportunities that these events created. Thank you.'

Yorkshire low-tech lad did good.

Cool.

What did I learn from my experience working collaboratively with this corporate giant?

I never really understood their organisation structure and where the people I met fitted into the project. Oracle employ 40 thousand people worldwide in a complex matrix structure. The people I met seemed to have two or even three bosses. It's not a world I normally inhabit.

Initially I was very nervous working with them, out of my normal comfort zone. They were very corporate in the way they operated, and I didn't initially find them very entrepreneurial.

They seemed really interested in my entrepreneurial research, as it was not a world they normally inhabit.

However they told me that Larry got the way entrepreneurs work. When anybody had a new business idea, they were allocated half a day a week to work on it. If it started looking interesting, then they were allocated more free time to work on it. If it became a new product Oracle would float off the idea and invest in it for a small stake.

Some of these spin-outs became billion-dollar business which Larry then bought back and added them into their portfolio, taking care not to corporatise them.

Larry Ellison clearly understands the entrepreneurial approach to developing a business.

Chapter Eighteen
Crafting Culture

I frequently find that, whilst some of my clients have a decent strategy or business plan, it is not supported by their culture. For example, if the plan is to sell more to existing customers, but instead of delighting them, they constantly let them down, their culture is not supporting their plan.

Culture was originally described as 'the way we do things here'. I prefer 'what people do when no one is looking'. This is the acid test of any culture.

The challenge facing businesses is how do you get all your people to behave in the ways you need to deliver your plan. And to get them to do this consistently.

You get culture by *design* (the one you want) or by *default* (the one you don't normally want).

Here is how I helped one client design their culture and it is a process I have shared successfully with dozens of businesses.

Keepmoat were an exemplar of how to establish a preferred culture, here is how they did it. They decided that their strategy, should be to sell more housing refurbishments to existing local authority customers. They proposed to do this by delighting them.

Our research showed that many public sector customers were fed up with construction companies letting them down and treating them without respect. They did not complete jobs on time, ripped them off on prices, delivered poor quality work and were rude to council tenants. We (I use the term *we* as I felt very much part of the process), decided to do the opposite and delight them, to achieve this, we needed to build a culture of Customer Delight.

See *Toolkit 3: Crafting Culture* and *Toolkit 5: Delighting Customers*.

Now you can imagine that when we announced our intensions to the bricklayers, joiners and electricians, it was not met with great enthusiasm.

'We are builders, we don't need this culture crap,' was a typical response.

Our reply was, 'We are going to do it and we need your help.'

The transformation of the typical construction attitudes took a major effort.

We had to give them a reason why they should bother helping us. This is the answer we gave them: 'our plan is to grow this business significantly over the next five years. This will require more directors, managers and supervisors. Our policy, as you know, is to promote from within so there will be lots of opportunities for those who are ambitious and want to develop their careers with us.'

This carrot seemed to go down well with most people. They could see there would be new opportunities to further their careers.

We decided on the values which would underpin the culture, and be non-negotiable, in order to delight customers.

We agreed the following:

- We will treat people with dignity and respect
- We will listen to and respond to our customers' needs
- Manage our business with integrity
- Deliver the highest quality service on time
- Take pride in being the best

Initially these were also met with cynicism, by many of the team.

The next phase was to get small groups of people from all levels in the business, labourers, foreman, managers, admin staff etc. to take each value and determine what they thought were the IN behaviours (what they wanted) and OUT behaviours (what they didn't want) for each value. For example: if we *treat people with dignity and respect*:

IN Behaviours	OUT Behaviours
Being considerate and respectful	Spreading rumours
Being empathetic	Interrupting people
Listen and engage with people	Breaking confidences
Respect confidences	Being rude to people

You might be surprised at the 'soft' behaviours that the teams came up with, we certainly were. Ironically the so called 'soft behaviours' should be renamed the hard behaviours, because they are hard to consistently stick to.

The point is the *team* came up with them and therefore *they* owned them.

But it didn't end there. We then got managers from each region across the UK to audit each other on whether they were behaving in line with the agreed behaviours. We called these cross-border audits.

Each region assessed another region, by interviewing people and looking for evidence of IN or OUT behaviours. They rated them out of ten on each behaviour. Initial scores varied from two to seven. Audits were carried out quarterly for two years and when the average scores reached eight plus, we stopped the audits. We knew the new culture was embedded. It had become 'just the way we do things here'.

The lessons learned we learned were: the business units were much tougher on auditing their colleagues than we might have been and they took it very seriously. Giving people ownership of their process pays dividends.

We found the builders on site, who were dealing with the council house tenants, were not helpful to them. They were often rude and aggressive and so consequently the tenants complained to their Local Authority. We decided it was a step too far to change the builders behaviour quickly, so we appointed female Tenant Liaison Officers, who handled the relationships with tenants with empathy. The tenants were delighted, with the way the ladies dealt with them and praised Keepmoat to the Local Authorities. This led directly to more work being secured.

Bingo!

Now you might be thinking that's an awful lot of work for a lot of people. Was it a distraction from their 'real' jobs? The culture change was to delight, rather than disgust customers. If we had not embarked on the culture change programme, the business would have carried on in the way they always did, competing on price like the rest of the industry.

Did it work?

It did. Keepmoat went on to become market leader in its sector dominating the competition and making record profits. Clearly it was not all down to this initiative, but the business recognised that it had made a significant contribution.

I will leave the last word to business owner Terry Bramall:

'David our culture is a major asset that has added real value to our business.'

Job done.

Chapter Nineteen
A mental health trust drives me crazy

Not every client project I take on is a raging success. But as I try to build my business, whenever I do anything new, I always get success or learning. I value both.

Early in my consulting practice, I responded to a request from a mental health trust in distress. I agreed to do the project pro bono.

It was a day I would come to regret.

The Trust was one of the worse performing in the country, with crippling financial problems.

To kick off the project I described my way of working with a cross section of people, to the CEO. I asked for high performers who had a track record of delivering results to work with me. They would be asked to use their knowledge and experiences of the trust to help improve its performance.

I was given a team of 'volunteers', all of whom I was informed, were keen, smart people who wanted to make a difference. They included nurses, supervisors, psychiatrists, doctors and a cross section of the Trust's administrative staff, twelve in all. My first impression was they were all smart and wanted to help the Trust with its problems.

The principle was that they knew where the opportunities were to boost the Trusts performance by working ON – making it better – as opposed to IN the organisation – making it work. See *Toolkit 1: Working ON the Business.*

It started well; the team came up with several opportunities to improve the financial performance. For example maintenance was outsourced to a local building company. They reviewed its standard rates for undertaking work, incredibly £35 for replacing two light bulbs, £156 for replacing a door handle. It was scandalous.

Other similar outsourcing rip-offs were investigated, and new providers were sourced, and this quickly reduced some costs.

But the scale of the losses could not be stemmed simply by reducing the costs of replacing light bulbs. So where were the big cost overruns?

Eventually the deputy CEO (the CEO is off with stress related illness), told me:

'The Blair government committed to improving the Health Service by engaging hundreds more consultants. This Trust has been given ten more highly paid consultants, which we do not need and cannot afford to pay, worse still there is no work for them to do.'

The wheels then started to come off our project. Four or five of my 'keen, smart team' started missing our meetings with no apologies. It was very frustrating. I asked what was happening.

'Oh, we are all so busy we have three or four meetings in the diary on the same day, at the same time. We decide on the day which to attend.'

I knew that Richard Branson operated in a similar fashion, he promised to attend a book launch of mine. He had sponsored the book, and then failed to turn up. His PA informed me, he would not make my meeting and apologised.

I said to my trust 'volunteers': 'Don't you ever think of informing the other meeting hosts that you will not be attending?'

'Oh no, it's just the way we do things here.'

I discovered that this was one of the worst managed organisations I had ever had the misfortune to work with. I don't doubt the professional staff's commitment to mental health, but none of them seemed to believe efficiency and cost control had anything to do with them.

I don't blame them because they suffered from a complete lack of leadership, so they focused solely on delivering their roles as healthcare professionals. 'Lions led by donkeys.'

Before I leave the project, I am determined to try to do something to try to help. So at the last meeting of my disparate group, we summarise together what they might do differently in the future, if they were trying to improve their organisation's efficiency.

Most feel they would like to have had a say, before being 'volunteered' for the project. They agree that attending meetings or sending a deputy in their place would be a respectful start. Not volunteering for actions that they did not have the time to deliver, was added to the list. They felt that senior managers should attend the first meeting, to reinforce the importance of the project, and that would create more engagement.

I copy this feedback into the senior management team. I get no response from them.

Regrettably, I sadly left the project with few successes, but the big costs that they really need sorting (reducing staffing levels, selling off assets etc.) were well above my pay grade. I hate it when I cannot help a client. At least I haven't added to their financial woes, as I offered my services for free. This project was in my learning, as opposed to success box.

Postscript

One month later the Trust CEO and Chair and several their board members were sacked, and the trust was put into special measures.

Chapter Twenty
'Winning' with Andy Forrester

'**D**avid, I am sorry** to have to tell you that Andy died last Friday.' This sad call was from Liz, Andy Forrester's wife.

Andy and I had worked together on projects on and off for twenty-six years. This sad call made me look back and reflect on our time together.

Andy Forrester was really very good at what he did. He had held several senior positions at LWT and the BBC for over forty years. He was a well-educated Scotsman living in Chiswick with an extensive network of friends and acquaintances in the London Labour party, including John Smith, Gordon Brown, Greg Dyke and others.

Andy could have been mistaken today for Jeremy Corbyn's twin brother: short in stature, receding thin grey hair, projecting nose and trimmed goatee beard. Like Corbyn he was a staunch Labour supporter. He also shared Corbyn's fashion sense: shabby, but not chic.

He began as an investigative journalist who migrated into producing and directing for London Weekend Television and then the BBC, before setting up his own production company, Lauderdale Productions.

I first met him in 1992 when having just been appointed producer of the new BBC series 'Winning', he interviewed me as the potential presenter. I was working in Scotland when he called me out of the blue to my great surprise:

'David, we would like you to present the new business series. Oh, and by the way you need to lose a couple of stone. It will look much better on TV.'

I learned that this was typical of his direct style.

WOW! I never expected this, having come away from the interview convinced I had screwed it up. Was I up to it? Would it be a flop? Despite my doubts I felt real excitement at my big chance.

Andy took a big risk in hiring someone who had no experience of presenting on TV and I will be forever grateful to him for putting his reputation as the producer, on the line.

He was kind, supportive and patient with me as I struggled to learn how to do my work in front of a camera.

A modest man, it was some time before I discovered that he had already won an impressive four BAFTA for his work. Certainly, working on the series with him was one of the most exciting things I have ever done.

'Winning' was a series of six half hour programmes demonstrating how small businesses succeed. At this time in 1992, Margaret Thatcher was one of the first Prime Ministers to champion the cause of business, although she favoured big business. Her favourite role model was Lord John King of British Airways.

Despite the focus on big corporations in this period, the importance of small businesses to the economy was starting to become recognised. An increasing number of people took the plunge and started their own business.

When running my own business, I was surprised to find that most of the business books and training programmes, for small businesses, were based on corporate structures and practice.

At that time Britain was still plagued with the idea that somehow old money was good, new money was 'dodgy'.

The BBC exploited this notion with comedy programmes such as

Minder and Only fools and Horses in which both Arthur Daley and Del Boy make money by people ripping off. As an entrepreneur myself, my clients were also in business, I took offence at the BBC's business output.

Young, passionate and naïve maybe, but I was deadly serious to put right what I saw as a serious wrong in British Society. My mission became: Help entrepreneurs to create great businesses.

My experiences led me to write my first book, *The Hallmarks for Successful Business*. Dinah Bennet, a mutual friend, gave a copy to Andy and that's how I got my screen test for the 'Winning' role.

I joined a team of experienced programme makers: researchers, directors, camera and sound people. I was amazed how quickly these individuals, who did not know each other, melded together as a team; much faster and more effectively than I was used to in the business world. Maybe it was the deadline pressure, or that they were used to being outcome focussed that enabled them to become productive so quickly?

I felt considerably out of my comfort zone but got I stuck in and gave it my best shot. I reflected later how much I had learnt whilst working with people from a different world to mine. For example, these cool people ate wraps and superfoods (yes, in 1992) which was all new to me. They dressed differently in jeans and T-shirts, typically with Che Guevara on the front, so I quickly dispatched my suit to the wardrobe.

I arrived carrying my briefcase which was dumped for a shoulder bag. Initially I felt like an outsider but over the six months of filming I gradually fitted in, maybe because I stopped asking for Yorkshire Tea and settled for their Earl Grey.

Also, I realised that, like me, they were experts in their fields and that we all needed each other to fulfil the project. There was one area of expertise that was entirely mine. In his role as producer Andy realised that the Series needed a more business content focus. In Series One I had co-written the scripts.

In Series Two Andy handed over the script writing to me and I also helped with editing; because, to my annoyance, the editors persistently cut out some of the key lessons for the business audience.

The series was designed was to select one topic per programme: customer service, leadership, marketing and so on. I was filmed interviewing a business owner who admitted to having a problem with the issue. Then we interviewed business owners, who showed how they successfully handled this. Finally, I then re-interviewed the original problem owner and asked what they had learnt from the experience of seeing how others had managed the issue well.

We were pleased with the responses from viewers, who contacted the BBC having watched the programmes, saying they intended to apply the lessons they had learned to their business.

My relationship with Andy was not always harmonious. For example, the first 'Winning' series Leadership programme won a BAFTA award for Business Programme of the Year in 1992, Andy forgot to tell me the date of the ceremony at the Royal Television Society. I discovered later the allocated seats were taken up by BBC executives who had contributed nothing to the series. I was bloody furious! My relationship with Andy changed from that day on, as my trust in him had dissipated for a while.

Later, when the series was completed and had been broadcast for the first time, Andy failed to inform me I was entitled to repeat fees. The series was repeated six times over the next three years. I never found out what happened to my share of the fees.

Nevertheless, I am grateful to Andy for giving me the opportunity to promote and raise the profile of small businesses on a national stage, each episode of 'Winning 1' averaged 2.5 million viewers.

I learnt some important lessons working on that series. I took a sabbatical from my business for four months, whilst doing the filming, appointing an MD, to run it whilst I was away. At the end of that experience I did not want to run the business anymore, so I sold it in 1994.

Andy handed me a 'once in a lifetime opportunity'. Did I grasp it with both hands? Well the series got record audiences from business viewers, but I never really exploited the opportunity to enhance my career. I could have hired a publicist (if I had known what one was back then) to build my brand and reputation. Instead I continued my consulting career and wrote three more books.

Andy and I worked together again on *Get Better or get Beaten*, a one off special for BBC 2, which won the Texaco Prize for the best business programme in 1994. Japanese quality management techniques such as Kaizen were very much in the media and Japans unique culture was thought to be the key to its success. The culture emphasised a commitment to working collaboratively in teams and to continuous improvement.

Andy and I decided to find out if it really was culture dependant. We identified two major British businesses, a film manufacturer, Ilford and the car maker, Rover, who had developed reputations for quality management. We revealed that they both had adopted the same Japanese techniques but with British managers. The culture myth was blown!

Later our roles were reversed somewhat. In 1999 Andy when he had extracted himself from the BBC bureaucracy and was having to bid for work I invited him to edit my book *In the Company of Heroes*, for me.

So, have attitudes changed much towards small businesses and entrepreneurs over the 25 years since we made the 'Winning' programmes? The word 'entrepreneur' appears to have a certain cachet with small business people, who appear proud to be called one. We have seen that with the people who join our local *For Entrepreneurs Only* support group.

The media generally are more positive towards entrepreneurs today. It's directors of corporates awarding themselves vastly inflated salaries and bonuses that occupy the negative media business headlines. In 2019 the average FTSE 100 CEO salary today is £5.3m which is 165 times more than a nurse, 140 times a teacher and 132 times a police officer. These ratios have increased dramatically over the past 25 years and are regularly reported in the media.

Has the BBC learned any lessons since Del Boy and Arthur Daly? Not entirely, they still promote opportunism on so called business shows such as *The Apprentice* and *Dragon's Den* both of which are filled with the get-rich-quick-by-being-on-telly brigade. This may be entertaining but the BBC's current commitment to showcasing real businesses and entrepreneurs is limited.

Back to Andy. I think on balance, his professionalism and his kindness, outweighed the issues that emerged between us.

Andy and I co-wrote my last book Entrecode in 2013.

He invited me to his birthday party in the same year, but I made some lame excuse and did not go. I never saw Andy again then Liz called me and informed me of his sad death.

A lesson for me; I really wish I had kept in touch better with those who have helped me along the way.

Andrew Forrester R.I.P.

Chapter Twenty-One
Winning TV Stories

In 1992 I co-wrote and presented the BBC TV business series 'Winning'. There were two series, each was six half hour programmes, on BBC2. We filmed some businesses who were flagging and others who were flying. The idea was to show the viewer the differences between them so they could learn from them.

In collaboration with the producer and director Andy Forrester we try to help and inspire struggling business to improve, using the businesses in the series as examples.

Here are some of the lessons we learned, from good, the bad and the ugly businesses we filmed.

We filmed an interesting business in Covent Garden. They manufactured and sold juggling balls, direct to customers in the market on a stall. Their clever selling point was that they also taught their customers how to juggle on the spot!

They were excellent at motivating their staff, a great example of what can be achieved by positive Leadership.

The 'Winning' film director suggested that I learnt how to juggle so I could introduce the business direct to camera, whilst juggling. I spent a few hours practising, but at the appointed time, the director thought it was a bit naff, so I didn't get to juggle on TV. I was very disappointed!

The business was called 'More Balls than Most'.

'More Balls' demonstrates the benefits of engaging the customer with the product in a fun and creative way. Customers are buying a new skill as well as three coloured balls. It puts a smile on customers faces which is unique.

So, how can you make your product an exciting new experience for your customers?

One struggling business we filmed made spectacle frames. The owner let's call him Ronnie was a chain-smoking alcoholic who insisted on showing me 'the Troubles' in Belfast, driving me around the no go areas in his silver Rolls Royce.

His car attracted a lot of attention from youths who decided to attack it with bricks and iron bars. Ronnie the owner sped off only to be stopped by the traffic lights that marked the border between Catholic and Protestant areas. The youths caught up with us. Oh God.

Ronnie wound down his window and started swearing at them. I screamed, 'Ronnie shut up and drive!'

'Bloody bastards, they need showing some manners!' he screamed.

'Yes, but not by us and definitely not right now.'

Ronnie was a character. He advice to his customers who complained that their spectacles had broken was, 'Well don't fucking sit on them.'

The next day, we were due to have lunch at his local golf club. Ronnie met me at his office, 'Sorry we can't go there for lunch. The IRA blew up the clubhouse this morning,' he announced without batting an eyelid.

I was pleased to get out of Belfast in one piece.

Ronnie was a one-man operation. He had several people working for him, but he refused to delegate anything and ran his business with an iron fist. It was totally dependent on him and he liked it that way.

He treated his customers and staff appallingly. How his business survived I have no idea. Sometimes characters can get away with being horrible because they are viewed as 'characters'. I wouldn't put up with Ronnie. Ronnie needs to 'let go to grow'.

I learned two years later that Ronnie had died of cancer and the business had folded.

We travelled to Bristol to film a business that manufactured 'street furniture' – street names on signs. They also made garage doors and American style car number plates.

My first impression was that, as a small business they had no real focus. They only made money from the garage doors, but that market was very competitive.

'Look great don't they,' James the owner's son proudly showed me the number plates 'Let me show you what they look like on my MG.'

Off he went. A few minutes later he screams to a halt in a bright red MG BT soft top, proudly displaying his American number plate.

Two of the secretaries told me, off camera, that James tried to impress them with his flash car, but they had rejected his advances.

James dismissed my suggestions that he might focus on the garage doors, where they were making money, and drop the street names and number plates which were frankly a distraction.

Like many struggling businesses they tried to solve their problems by diversifying away from their problems. We used this business to illustrate poor leadership.

Sadly, I learned two years later that the business had gone bust.

Mick Lee runs a security business based in South Yorkshire called Constant Security. It provides professional security services to a whole range of clients across the UK, including most of the racecourses and some football clubs.

Mick is a 25 stone bruiser who looks like 'Desperate Dan' in the comics. He is always smartly dressed in a pinstripe suit which together with his build, he says creates confidence in an industry, renowned for cowboys.

'We are one of the few security firms that has the British Standard for Quality Assurance. This helps our clients to sleep easy in their beds when we are looking after their property,' Mick explains.

'We give clients peace of mind because our people always look and behave properly,' he enthuses as we film him entertaining his clients at Doncaster Racecourse with his wise-cracking Yorkshire humour.

Mick has built a successful business by carefully vetting his security people, training and managing them in a professional manner. He understands what clients really want from a security business and he ensures he provides it. He is a good example of somebody who has built a business in a competitive market by getting the basics right and not cutting corners. He is a Winner.

Thomson and Morgan are the UK's largest seed and plant providers. Started in Ipswich in 1855 by William Thomson, the son of a local baker who was fascinated by growing plants from seed in the shops back garden. He built a business selling seeds from three outlets in Ipswich.

He was joined by John Morgan, a shrewd businessman, who was able to offer sound financial knowledge and the capital to enable the expansion of the business to be soundly financed.

The Marketing Director tells me, 'We take the mystery out of gardening practices. We have grown the business using imaginative marketing practices. We have a reputation that if a grower wants a seed from anywhere in the world, we probably have it.'

This is a well managed operation that has successfully grown (literally) from a back garden in a shop to an international enterprise over 165 years. The business grew by getting good people into key roles and 'sticking to the knitting' not diversifying into areas where they don't have the expertise.

This is a good lesson for other's who may be tempted to diversify their operations into other products where they don't have the expertise or the benefit of years of experience.

These are examples of some of the good and poor businesses we presented on the 'Winning' series. The idea was to show the viewer both good and bad businesses and let them see the difference between the two.

Interestingly most of the business viewers who contacted the BBC, said they felt were more like our poor examples, than the good guys.

Very Worrying.

Chapter Twenty-Two
Cracking the Code

I wait at Doncaster railway station for the arrival of the London train. Wyatt Woodsmall should be on it, but it's running late.

A visit to America and meeting Wyatt, had proven to be a turning point in my quest to crack the entrepreneurial code.

But first, let me rewind a bit.

One of life's great mysteries is how entrepreneurs create great businesses, often from practically nothing.

If we don't know, how then do we help others become successful?

Why does it matter?

Entrepreneurs create the wealth that pays the taxes that enable civilised societies to function. They also provide employment to people enabling them to earn a living. Without entrepreneurs all we have is bureaucracy, costs and chaos.

My work involves helping entrepreneurs to succeed, but if I don't know how they do it how can I help them?

I decide to try to crack the entrepreneurial code. But in my endeavours, I hit a brick wall, when I ask entrepreneurs how they create a successful business they usually shrug their shoulders and say, 'Dunno, I just do it.' This is not much help, so I needed to find a way to help them.

It was this quest to find the key to the entrepreneurial mind that led me to meet Wyatt Woodsmall in Washington DC.

'David the mystery can be solved by using the science of High Performance.'

'Oh good but what's that Wyatt?'

He convinced me, by telling me some amazing stories how he worked with the American Olympic team Gold medal winners, working out how they did it and then sharing those precious insights with other team members.

On my return to the UK I raised 100k from government sources, matched it with my own money and arranged to bring Wyatt to the UK, to help me crack the code.

So, here I am today, on Doncaster railway station waiting for Wyatt, to begin our journey of discovery.

The train arrives and I watch as a massive trunk suitcase is disgorged followed gingerly by Wyatt. Looks like he is staying with us for months rather than the six weeks we agreed. We shake hands and I greet him warmly, 'Wyatt, welcome to Doncaster.' I am excited about beginning our quest.

We are up early the next day and ready to go. I begin by describing my frustration.

'When I ask entrepreneurs how they create success they just give me a blank look and shrug their shoulders.'

Wyatt explains in his gravelly baritone, 'that's because they are unconsciously competent. This means they have worked out how to do things, usually by trial and error, but can't explain in a useful way how they do it. This makes it impossible to help others.'

'So, Wyatt if we help them describe how they do things, it could have a massive positive impact on other entrepreneurs and the economy overall.'

'Yep, that's the prize, David.'

Our plan is to interview successful entrepreneurs in the Yorkshire Region, with Wyatt using his unique Behavioural Modelling interviewing process.

At the first interview Wyatt asked his questions and the interviewees unburdened themselves, as Wyatt madly scribbled notes.

We completed three interviews in the first day. Had it gone well, I wondered?

'We got some interesting stuff today, much food for thought.'

We retired back to my house.

Having Wyatt living with us full time was proving challenging, particularly for Ellen. Wyatt drank three litres of full fat coke a day and smothered all his meals with half a container of tomato ketchup. That was the good bit. Wyatt seemed to have borrowed somebody else's teeth, as he ate like a cement mixer, sharing his food with us, along with his spittle. Lovely.

We have now been interviewing entrepreneurs for three weeks. As we talk, after the interviews, I begin to understand the process of Behavioural Modelling and start to see a pattern emerging in the entrepreneur's behaviour. We collected copious notes.

'What do you reckon our next stage is, Wyatt?'

'We need to make sense of it, search for the threads and join up the dots.'

'My initial observations are that successful entrepreneurship is much more of a personal than a business process. For example: getting in the zone, having a positive attitude, staying persistent, seems much more important than some of the traditional business stuff like market research, planning or bookkeeping.'

'I get that, Wyatt.'

'World class athletes have known this for years, most of the winners have mind coaches, they practice getting in zone and staying positive. The difference between Gold medal winners and the rest is not diet or fitness it's in the mind.'

'We have not cracked the code yet Wyatt, but we do have some new surprising new insights, so what's next?'

He responds, 'I suggest we go back to Washington and analyse all the data we have and try to develop a new model of entrepreneurial behaviour.'

'Right lets, do it.'

Off I shoot to Washington.

Wyatt and I spent 5 days analysing the data we collected at his home. A distraction for me were his three cats jumping all over me. I hate bloody cats.

'It's clear, David, that our initial observations about the process were well founded. Entrepreneurship is very much a personal process. We now need to create a model that explains our findings and we need a name for it to give it an identity.'

Trying to find an appropriate name took us two days: the entrepreneur's bible, the E process, successful entrepreneurs, none of these felt right.

I asked, 'What are we trying to do here?'

'Well it's about entrepreneurs and how they do things, a kind of code I suppose.'

'How about: The Entrepreneur's Code?'

'Too wordy and not memorable.'

'Okay how about, Entrecode?'

'It's not a proper word.'

'I know, that's the bloody point, we have created something that did not exist, so there can't by definition be a word to describe it!'

At 5.15 on the 22nd of October 2002 the Entrecode was born.

I was mighty relived to be leaving Washington DC today. I spent the last few days unable to leave my hotel because the area was in lockdown due to a sniper that killed 17 people. Eventually, when the police arrest the killer, John Allen Mohammed, I escape to the airport. Thank Fuck.

I am sat in my office 17 years later with a client and friend Mike Rice reflecting on the Entrecode experience.

'Do you believe you cracked the code David?'

'Entrepreneurs who see it believe we have.'

The late Allan Gibb, internationally respected Emeritus Professor of Small Business at Durham University Business school, believes we have, but thinks Entrecode might be mistaken for a beef steak!

'What did you do to promote it, David?'

'I presented the Entrecode to the World Entrepreneurs Forum in Los Angeles. The audience consisted of academics from around the world, public sector leaders and Entrepreneurs from Silicon Valley. I was very nervous about a lad from Yorkshire telling the Silicon Valley high flyers about entrepreneurship!

'The responses were very different. The academics queried my research sample size, which is common practice, and why it had not been peer reviewed. It went straight over the heads of the public sector people.

'Several entrepreneurs came to me afterwards saying they really got it and it explained for the first time how they did business as they never found the traditional business school stuff much help.

'One lady came up to me in tears and said "My husband and I built our business, Sage Publications, in just the way you described, unfortunately he passed away last year, but you reminded me of all the things we did together. Thank You."

'I published a book of our findings 'Entrecode – unlocking the entrepreneurial DNA' to good reviews and acclaim from entrepreneurs.

'Saville Consulting, a global psychometric provider and I collaborated and produced a psychometric test: *The Entrepreneurial Potential Report.*

This assesses an individual's potential on the key Entrecode factors. This is now used in several countries and surprisingly Russia is a big user.

'I also built an Entrecode website and hired a PR agency to promote it.'

'Get off your soapbox mate and tell me honestly are you satisfied with the results after nearly 20 years?' Mike says.

'Well, we certainly shone a light on the fact that it's much more of a personal than a business process. When I present it to entrepreneurs, they seem to get it, as if somebody understands how they do things at last.

'The EPR psychometric is now used in at least 20 countries.

'But the book never really took off, very disappointing, as was the website, although I invested 20k promoting it.'

'What would you differently next time?'

'Spend more time putting the book together, and open up our research findings to peer review by a respected academic, to validate the results independently.'

'Was it worth the effort?'

'Certainly, it was great learning experience, but unfortunately I was satisfied knowing how entrepreneurs do it, I didn't shout about it and deliver the transformational opportunities for other entrepreneurs I believe it could have done.'

The Entrecode:

Getting into the Zone
Drive, Compelling Vision, Goal Directed Energy, Action Orientation.

Joining the dots
Passion, Networking, Creating Partnerships.

Seeing possibilities
Strategic Mindset, Options Thinking, Savvy.

Creating Opportunities
Customer Focus, Problem seeking – problem solving, Synthesis.

Staying in the zone
Focus, Positive Mindset, Persistence.

Building Capability
Teamworking, Installing systems, Continuous learning.

Chapter Twenty-Three

Stormy weather at the Met Office

I started an exciting project working with the Met Office in Exeter. They had been instructed by their government paymasters to become more commercial and earn fees directly from private clients to support their central funding. My task was to help them win private sector clients.

As part of my introduction to the organisation, two men in white coats (coming to take me away?) take it in turns to brief me on the organisation.

Stand by for some interesting facts:

'We get a call every morning at 8am from the Queen's Equerry: "Will Her Majesty require an umbrella today?"' Delivered with a broad grin.

And: 'Before our armed forces go into any theatre of war, we forecast the weather within a hundred metres' radius of where they are, anywhere in the world.'

And: 'We can identify and track any ship anywhere, by its wake. We can also track submarines.'

'We are regarded,' a pause for dramatic effect, 'as having the best weather forecasting service in the world. Along with the Americans.'

I am impressed. This is a highly successful organisation that simply needs to learn to sell its expertise, which may not prove easy, because it's always been funded by the government and has no experience of creating commercial deals.

Apparently, they had taken the instruction from the government too literally and were in the process of offering their unique technology to some 'friendly countries' like Russia and China. The military top brass got wind of this approach and quickly canned it. I picture the scene: 'Hey old boy, we can't go selling our secrets to the Ruskies…'

Starting the assignment in my usual way, I prepare to select a small team of internal people who could help develop this project. I set about interviewing members of staff who, it is suggested, might fit my requirements: entrepreneurial, innovative – and up for the challenge.

The first candidate, a young sales manager, proves disconcerting. She turns up in a low cut blouse and sporting crimson pouty lipstick.

She gets straight to the point. 'I've been at the Met Office for three years, and before you ask, I haven't actually made any sales yet – but I'm working on it. No, I don't want to fill in your questionnaire. I am starving and I need a Mars bar.' She stands up and leaves.

I don't want her on the team.

It continues downhill from here. I discover only one candidate who meets my specification – we need several. Experience tells me that if you don't get the right people 'on the bus' at the start, the project is doomed to failure. My preferred way of working, by finding and unleashing the talent from within, is unlikely to work here.

On reflection, the shift in culture that the Met Office is seeking – from high-tech public-sector culture to commercial sales operation – will almost certainly require the recruitment of new people with appropriate commercial skills and experience. It is usually the hardest change leaders must make.

Many underestimates the challenges posed by trying to radically change their culture, often with dire consequences.

I discuss these issues with the Met Office management, and we agree to put the project on the back burner, whilst they figure out a way forward.

You can't win them all.

Postscript

2007. The sales manager, now a 'global brand consultant', later wins Lord Alan Sugar's *Apprentice*, but rejects his job offer. So, my claim to fame is I that turned her down and Lord Sugar offered her a job!

Chapter Twenty-Four
'My kind of Consultant'

I was interviewed by Grahame King, a journalist from the Newcastle Journal, about my work as a management consultant. I was due to deliver a talk to businesses in Newcastle and this was part of the PR for the event.

I am usually embarrassed talking about myself and my work. However this gave me a chance to promote my conviction that management is a profession, that should be taken more seriously.

We met at the Journal's office in Newcastle. Grahame is tall, slim, maybe in his thirties. He greets me with a 'not another business guru look'. He has a tape recorder and a pad and uses both throughout the interview, which lasts for over an hour. Think I was right to be nervous....

'Professor Hall, what kind of consultant are you?'

'Please call me David. There are three kinds of consultant: the technical expert hired for their specialist expertise; the analyst who reviews a business and disappears; and the facilitator who works with the business to help them solve their problems. I get most satisfaction from being a facilitator.'

'What kind of satisfaction?'

'Generally the wisdom to make an organisation successful resides within it. I work with the CEO to help them to find the wisdom and then support them to develop the business and the people. It works when you get it right. The organisation and the managers grow and it's cost effective. I love it when the process delivers the results the client is seeking.'

'Does your approach always work, and if not, why not?'

This guy is very direct.

'Well if we get all the ingredients in place it works; if the CEO is serious about making a change, if we find the internal talent that are released to work on the business, if they are keen and get on with it. When any of these factors are missing it doesn't work.'

'Is having good managers important?'

'You've got me on my favourite topic now Grahame. It has been estimated that ninety per cent of organisational problems in both the private and public sector are down to poor management. My job is to help managers to do their work well.'

'Your business card reads Professor David Hall. Are you an academic?'

'I got the Professorship for my lifetime work with entrepreneurs, from the Curtin Business in School Perth, Australia. I'm not an academic, I'm a consultant who tries to use the latest research evidence in my work. I am sometimes seen as an academic by business people and a populist by academics. I walk the tightrope between these two polar opposites.'

'How many businesses have you worked with in your career so far, David?'

'I happened to look at that the other day. More than ninety.'

'What would you like to be remembered for?'

'As a student of entrepreneurs who tries to help them, their businesses and society. Does that sound a bit grandiose?'

'No it sums up what you have been doing. Thanks for your time David.'

Grahame was professional, a bit cold, no jokes or asides, just here to get the job done.

I was a bit nervous about what he would write about me. He didn't give much away and was difficult to read, so I waited anxiously to discover in the Journal what he had written about me. Here is his opening and his summary:

I am meeting Professor David Hall today with a degree of trepidation. Although he claims to dislike the term guru, it has found its way onto his blog emailed to me ahead of our meeting, albeit from a third party. So I am on my guard.

He is casually dressed and speaks with a broad Yorkshire accent. Both these facts do a solid job in disarming my cynicism. There is no suit, or knuckle-crushing handshake and no exaggerated interest in, or flattery of, the newspaper, as some of the guru genus have been known to indulge in. Of course, this may be Hall's schtick – his ordinariness – and I have fallen for his charm, or it maybe he is a relaxed individual.........

His Summary; David Hall has done it all since leaving school at 16 – worked for a plc, built his own business, sold it, written books, made a BAFTA award 'Winning' TV series, become a professor and helped over ninety businesses survive, change or grow.

He is my kind of consultant.

And Grahame you are my kind of journalist!

He got me better than any Journalist I have met.

Thank you, Grahame.

Chapter Twenty-Five
Classroom entrepreneur

Chris Keating's business card reads 'Christopher Keating, boss of CJ Scanners'.

I met him at my daughter's school prize giving. We were talking afterwards, and he told me,

'When I started my business, I wanted to offer a service for people, offering a very personal design and printing service for their high-quality stationary. I do all the design work myself as well as the printing and administration. It's a one-person business....for now!'

You might think there is nothing remarkable about Chris, so here is a copy of the quotation for a small printing job, he sent my daughter:

Dear Miss Penny Hall

I am writing to you with a quote for the thirty colour letter heads which comes to £5.

I hope you find it reasonable. I enclose the different types of paper you can have at no extra cost.

To see the designs, arrange to meet me in the form room at dinner.

Yours sincerely

Chris Keating

You see Chris, was just eleven years old. He was in Penny's class. He has launched his business whilst still at school and was deadly serious about it. But how did he get started?

'I saved up one hundred pounds from my Christmas and birthday and used it to buy a scanner. I started to do scanning jobs for people. Before long people were asking me to design and produce letterheads, business cards and leaflets.

At school I carry my sales brochure, order pad and samples in my satchel and show them to people in the school dining room.'

I discover that his business is now not just confined to customers at school. He won a contract to produce the local parish magazine and was making a modest profit.

'I am going to reinvest my profits in better equipment and a new computer so I can offer a better service.'

Why did Chris start his business?

'My mum and dad split up when I was five, I didn't like either of them, so I went to live with my granny, who has looked after me ever since. We don't have a lot of money, so I decided that I would do something to help.'

One thing was clear, this is not a schoolboy doing favours for friends or running a hobby. Chris was so serious about his business he booked himself on a business start-up course in his summer holidays with a group of adults. To look the part, he insisted his grandmother had his suit cleaned and pressed.

And Chris also learned some of the basic entrepreneurial attitudes. When my daughter, a well organised person, offered to help him with his invoicing, he replied,

'Thank you but this is a one-person business at present, so I need to keep my costs under control. But can I interest you in some invitation cards for your birthday party next month, designed especially for you?'

Chris reminded me of another schoolboy entrepreneur who established a well-known business.

Postscript

20 years later Chris is Customer Experience Manager at Arriva Rail London.

Chapter Twenty-Six

'Delighting Customers' at Bonar Flotex

I take a call from a Peter Bartlett. He announced himself as the CEO of a company called Bonar Flotex, who manufacture carpet tiles.

'Mr Hall, I read your piece today in Management Today, on "Delighting Customers" and I wondered if you would be prepared to visit us and give us some feedback on our service?'

In the article I argued that going the extra mile for customers and seeking to 'Delight' them normally leads to, high levels of repeat business, referrals to new customers and a lowering of sensitivity to price. Most sane businesses would take these benefits.

I was intrigued by his call, so I arranged to meet him. He promised to send me a map to help me find their factory, which was in Derbyshire. The next day the map duly arrived, but this was no ordinary map. It directed me from my home right to his office door. It was large scale, easy to follow and very helpful in the days before Satnav!

So today I am off to meet Mr Bartlett.

I arrive at the security building, by the factory gate. A security guard appears.

'Morning, Mr Hall, did you have a good trip sir? Could you please park your car in the bay next to reception?' (How did he know my name?)

The allotted car space is right next to the reception door. I am surprised to see my name on a board announcing: 'Reserved for Mr David Hall'. This is very unusual. Normally this car parking space is reserved for the CEO or Chairman.

It gets better. The receptionist greets me with a big smile 'Good morning, Mr Hall, did you have a good journey here today?'

'Er yes thank you,' I mumble, wondering how she knew my name.

'Right, Mr Hall, please take a seat and Mr Bartlett will be with you shortly.'

'Mnm don't you need me to sign in?'

'Oh no, that's being taken care of.'

As my bum hits the seat a door opens and a young man carrying a black coffee and two chocolate biscuits on a silver tray comes in. He carefully places the tray down in front of me.

'Good morning, Mr Hall.' (How the fuck does he know my name and how does he know I have a black coffee and two chocolate biscuits for my morning break?) 'Mr Bartlett will be with you in a moment.'

This is now getting beyond bloody belief. I start looking around to see if have been set up on 'You've Been Framed'.

I'm now checking my watch.

Sure enough, after 2 minutes, bang on time, another door opens and in walks a smartly dressed man with a big smile, holding out his hand in a friendly gesture.

'Good morning, Mr Hall. Did you find us okay?'

'Yes, thank you, Mr Bartlett.'

'Please call me Peter. May I call you David?'

Now, when I am trying to interest people in Delighting Customers, I usually begin by asking what their customer service is like.

Normally the answer is: Ugh, erm, what do you mean?

Now, reflect a moment on my experiences with Bonar Flotex so far: helpful map, pleasant security guard who knows my name, car park space at reception, receptionist who also knows my name, coffee as I like it on arrival, meeting starts spot on time; this is not the norm....

So, I was not surprised when Peter responded to my question with, 'Shall we start with delivery. Do you want year to date, this month, this week or today?'

And so, it went on. They had measures on every aspect of their customer service.

Their performance was outstanding.

Peter looked at with a big smile on his face. 'You want to know how we managed to Delight you on your arrival don't you?'

He moved towards me with a broad grin.

'Well, our customers told us we were pretty good at customer service, but we wanted to be better, to turn it into our competitive advantage. So, we got our team together: security, reception, admin, and sales and asked how we could Delight our customers.

'Out of that exercise came the idea that when people are coming for meetings at the factory, we call their secretary and ask what type of car they drive, the registration number and how they take their drinks. We ask them to keep it to themselves, as we want to surprise them.

This is communicated internally to all our people and on the day, it happens as if by magic. The experience normally puts a smile on the customer's face.'

'Well, Peter, it blew my socks off, now remind me why you wanted to talk to me about your customer service.'

Peter howled with laughter and I left, promising I would never ever buy carpet tiles from anyone other than Bonar Flotex.

And that's the point.

Postscript

I used the Bonar Flotex story in my presentations and consultancy projects since visiting Peter Bartlett's business. Many other businesses have been inspired by how they created competitive advantage by delighting their customers. It has proven to be a very effective way of competing. See *Toolkit 4: Getting Customer Service Right* and *Toolkit 5: Delighting Customers*.

'Delighting Customers' was a concept introduced by Tom Peters in his groundbreaking book *In Search of Excellence*, first published in 1982. His research discovered that by providing excellent customer service businesses enjoyed the benefits of high levels of repeat business, new business from referrals and a lowering of sensitivity to price.

Chapter Twenty-Seven

Alberts Engineering

Having been impressed by Bonar Flotex, I am off up the A1 to see another potential client, based in Gateshead on Tyneside. Let's call them Alberts Engineering.

It's pouring with rain as I arrived at the gates of the engineering works. I can see the security guard sheltering from the weather in his white hut. I sit in my car, waiting to see if he will brave the rain. Of course he will. It's his job, isn't it? And so begins a game regularly played with security guards called 'who gets wet'....

I start looking very obviously at my watch, trying to give him the hurry up. No such luck. He grimaces at me and takes another drag on his cigarette. A big fat guy with short cropped hair, he looks more like a villain than somebody entrusted with the security of the place. Should he be smoking on duty?

Okay. I lose. I get out of the car, and the conversation then goes something like this:

'I've come to see Mr Smith. My name is David Hall, you've probably heard of me.' (Okay, I didn't say the last bit.)

He grunts and looks at his clipboard. 'Hall you say. You're not down here, son.' He sounded triumphant so I pull out my letter of invitation, rain trickling down inside my collar.

He grimaced, picked up the phone. 'Hall, yes. Says he has an appointment.'

He drops his voice. 'While you're on, darlin', can you get me a copy of the Mirror and a packet of cheese and onion crisps? Yes, I know I owe you for the pie yesterday. Cheers, love.' He puts the phone down with a smirk.

'Yes,' he says reluctantly, 'apparently you do have an appointment.'

'Thank you. So where should I park?'

'Oh, not round here son, you can see what it's like, more than my job's worth. There's an NCP car park about three hundred yards down on the left,' he says, pointing.

Cheers. Thank you so much.

Two thoughts: if he calls me son again – he is at least thirty years younger than me – I will thump him; secondly, I am going to get even wetter, as I have no raincoat.

I eventually park my car and then go in search of the reception. It is small and uninviting, in need of a good tidy up.

'Good morning. My name is David Hall and I have…'

'Have you got an appointment?' the receptionist, barks without looking up from her screen. She looks bored and unhappy, in her faded company shirt.

'Look, I have just been through all this with the gorilla on the gate.'

'Hall, you said?' She is still staring at her computer screen. 'Take a seat. Mr Smith will be with you shortly.'

Desperate for a coffee, I wait – another thirty minutes.

Mr Smith is a small man, shabbily dressed, with unkempt hair.

'Right, Mr Hall what can you do for my business?' he asks, folding his arms tightly across his chest in the 'I am not listening to you' position.

'Well, Mr Smith, my brief is to help businesses develop their customer service and delight their customers. May I ask how you would judge your company's customer service?'

'We don't get many complaints.'

'Mr Smith, with respect, if you're judging your customer service by the number of complaints you get, you may be missing the point. Many customers don't complain. Research shows that they'll simply take their business elsewhere and then tell at least five people why they've done that.'

He glares at me. I plough on.

'If you scrutinised your staff, could you identify anyone who may be turning off customers? They can lurk anywhere in your business' – I pause for effect – 'from security to reception.'

My point is lost on him.

'We nickname them Sales Prevention Officers.'

'We don't have any of them here, laddie. I'd bloody well sack them.'

It doesn't take long to figure out that trying to help this business was a non-starter. The service problem starts right at the top. I make my excuses and leave.

This is a poor business. I didn't need to see their accounts to know it is struggling. From this brief encounter, the company culture clearly falls well below acceptable levels. Sometimes you just must walk away.

What did I learn from this experience?

Firstly, the difference between Alberts Engineering and Bonar Flotex is stark. One delights its customers; the other disgusts them.

It also reminds me that the strengths and weaknesses of the business mirrors the leader's attitude and behaviour. That's why the selection of the leader is a critical business decision.

The company culture is the most important part of its identity – its brand.

Branding is not just about designing a great logo or website; ultimately, people judge a business by its integrity and values.

Right: it is time to be honest. Is your business like Alberts Engineering, or Bonar Flotex?

Chapter Twenty-Eight
Matt's media magic

One definition of madness is to do nothing differently and yet expect things to get better. That's just vain hope.

So it's really rewarding when clients take the actions, we agree upon to develop their business; equally, it's bloody frustrating when they do nothing. They roll out the usual excuses – 'been busy'; 'needed to sort some things'; 'been off with a cold'. I've heard them all.

Of course, sometimes people do have legitimate reasons for their inaction, but most often they simply have not got around to it.

Whilst I'm venting my frustrations, I'll mention another situation that drives me crazy: when I have provided clients with a Toolkit (a process map), for them to follow in order to improve their business) and they tell me that it has not worked.

I questioned one client recently about his company's progress.

'Did you follow Step One and talk to your key customers?'

'No. We know them well enough already.'

'So how about Step Two? Did you ask those four questions precisely, as we discussed?'

'Well, we kind of adapted them.'

And so it went on. It turned out that they had not followed the process and then wondered why it had not worked for them. Unbelievable.

So, it's fantastic when a client like Matt Dass of Eon Visual Media shows up one day, proffering an expensive bottle of Champagne and thanking me for my help. It's very unusual to be thanked in my job, so I welcomed his gratitude – and the Bollinger!

Matt is one of the good guys who runs his own business. He is smart, polite and receptive. He is also very fit. He runs marathons for fun.

Matt's business is in app development, animation, design and video production; he employs 20 people and has an impressive list of clients. He told me about his business at our first meeting and it became clear he had three main goals: to manage his costs better, to generate more business and make more profit.

His biggest cost is hiring out technical staff, selling their time on projects. Logging their hours was a key issue and it transpired he did not record or know how well they time managed. I introduced him to a law firm whose paranoia about time recording meant they had a fool proof system. Matt adopted their process and his business average charge out rate went up from 55% to 90%. Consequently his profits increased dramatically.

To generate more business, I introduced Matt to a company who created new sales by 'partnering', which involves building strong, mutually beneficial relationships with selected clients. Once again Matt adopted the new approach and his sales to existing clients improved. He is now working on creating new clients.

Matt is a good learner with a positive open mind and a 'can-do' attitude: he deserves the success he created.

The key point here is that most clients have two or possibly three problems they need to solve. However, they are usually up to their necks in their day-to-day business and can't see the wood for the trees. They often feel they are wrestling with too many problems and don't deal successfully with any of them.

The good news is that, with the right focus, three problems can be resolved (seventeen can't be!) and what's more, as in Matt's case, the solutions usually lift the whole mood and spirit of the business. Another significant benefit.

A further point: whenever a business presents with a problem, I have usually dealt with that issue or something similar with previous clients. By connecting the two clients through an introduction, they frequently solve the problem between themselves – a form of mentoring. This is especially effective when working with entrepreneurs who prefer to get their learning from other like-minded entrepreneurs – people who have been there and done it – rather than from reading books, attending training courses, or (dare I say it?) consulting consultants!

By the way, Matt's Champagne was enjoyed by Ellen: I prefer beer.

Chapter Twenty-Nine

Book launch at the Groucho

My second book: *In the company of Heroes* was launched at the Groucho Club in Dean Street, London. My publishers Kogan Page suggested this venue because 'that's where we can get the business journalists to turn out for a free drink.'

The launch is held in a private room; drinks and canapés flowing. The publisher assured me we had succeeded in getting the right media to the event. My friend Andy Forrester, a former journalist, had said, 'I will invite my best mate, Greg Dyke, he has just been appointed as Director General of the BBC, so will be a great attractor for the business media.'

He is.

One female journalist from the Evening Standard, who clearly was enjoying the free cocktails, harangued me, jabbing her finger hard into my chest: 'You bloody authors are all the same suggesting a big name will turn up (Greg Dyke) to get us here and they never appear.'

I was shocked, having never personally experienced the charm of national media journalists.

Ten minutes later Andy walked in with Greg Dyke. The assembled journalists rushed over to interview him. I looked across the room at the Evening Standard lady, caught her eye, nodded in Greg's direction and smiled. Oh joy. She looked peeved and staggered out drunk shortly after.

I had assumed that Kogan Page were paying for the Groucho Gig, until the Groucho manager thrust a bill into my hand, as I was about to leave. Another lesson for a naïve author, publishers do fuck all, the author does everything and then has the pleasure of paying for all the marketing and PR.

Nice job publishing.

There was a benefit that I got from this event. Two businesses that were at the launch approached me and asked if I would be interested in helping them. Both turned into interesting projects that more than paid for the book launch.

Chapter Thirty
Carpets fitted

I emerge from a sleepless night, worrying about what mischief the carpet fitters will be up to today.

This obviously requires a bit of elaboration.

Ten years ago, we moved to a new house in Bawtry. I am put in charge of organising the carpet fitting. We arrived with much excitement and opened our new front door.

The new carpets had been laid, but the fitters had left enough off cuts, strewn everywhere, to fill a large skip. They had also taken all the internal doors off and left them lying around. Bastards.

It took two hours of clearing up before we could move in.

I protested to my wife, 'But darling, you did instruct me get the cheapest quote.'

Charlie's Carpets had been the cheapest, but I didn't realise I was hiring Charlie bloody Chaplin!

This was not my finest hour.

Today, ten years on, we are moving again. Once again, I am delegated responsibility for organising the carpet laying. Ellen's words ring in my ears: 'Right, you're in charge of carpets and I don't want a repeat of the last fiasco.'

I use all my contacts to find a decent carpet fitter. Eventually I choose a local carpet company; let's hope they live up to the recommendations.

Ten days later we arrive at our new house and with much trepidation. I open the front door…

Not a carpet off-cut insight in sight. No evidence of the work, other than beautifully fitted carpets wall to wall.

And all the doors are in place. Hallelujah.

Now, is this just good customer service or is it customer delight?

I believe it's customer service. I paid for it therefore I expect it to be done.

Ellen shouts out and I rush over….

There's a bouquet of flowers, on the table and she's reading the card: 'Dear Mrs Hall. Welcome to your new home Best Wishes, your carpet fitters.'

Now, *that's* customer delight. Unexpected, not paid for and beyond the norm.

Delighting customers is a great way to compete because you will stand out from the competition. See Toolkit 5: Delighting Customers.

If you delight your customers you will enjoy; repeat business from customers, referrals to potential customers and price will be less of an issue.

Most sane business people will take these benefits.

Chapter Thirty-One

The Magic of Mantras

I gave a talk to a well-known bank's Business Managers' Group (BMG for short) in Durham. Topic: 'The Magic of Mantras'.

The bank wants to help their business managers understand how entrepreneurs think, so that they can work more closely with them as clients.

The meeting was held at Durham business school's conference centre. I arrived early and met some of the delegates for coffee before we got started. There are forty delegates plus some of the teaching faculty, who had organised the event.

I begin my talk with a definition:

'The origins of mantras are in Hinduism and Buddhism.: A mantra is a repeated word or sound often used to aid concentration, particularly in meditation. I use a mantra in my daily meditation but was advised to keep it to myself.

'A mantra is used today as a rallying call to action, for people to get behind the priorities of their business. A mantra creates a business's DNA, the glue that unites strategy, culture and people's behaviours.'

'Can you give us an example of a mantra?' asks a lady in the front row.

'Okay. This simple mantra, for example, means we should collaborate internally and not compete or play power games.' I write *One Team* in large letters on the flip chart.

'Here's another. *Let Go to Grow* gives people licence to delegate and concentrate on the critical parts of their own role.' I look back at the audience, marker pen in hand. 'If the CEO and senior team share the mantras with colleagues and consistently model that behaviour themselves, then most people generally will follow their lead.'

'Isn't that a kind of brainwashing?', a lecturer chips in.

I think for a moment. 'No. It's a simple way of letting people know what's expected of them.'

I continue, 'At the start of a project, the mantra might be this.' I scribble *Brutal honesty in the assessment of the business* across the paper.

'The aim is to encourage people to get the facts, identify true causes of problems and don't fool themselves.

'When the priority is to improve business performance, a useful mantra is: *Work ON as well as IN the businesses.* This means focussing effort on trying to improve the way things are done in the business.'

'Once a business sorts itself out, are mantras obsolete as a tool?' asks a guy sitting on the back row. (They're still awake, then!)

I shake my head. 'When my best client, a building company called Keepmoat, had worked out its strategy and was making outstanding profits, they adopted a new mantra: *Keep going!*

'Mantras have proved to be effective in helping to translate priorities into action, in a way that everyone in the business can get behind.'

I pause, then ask, 'Has your business got a mantra?'

A young lady replies. 'I think it's *Look after customers.*

'Do you all do that?' I ask

A few nervous coughs and eyes cast down, 'We... er... try,' she replies nervously looking around at her colleagues.

The host draws the event to a close, as the next speaker is ready.

'Thanks, David, I need to work on our mantra at the business school,' he says with a laugh

As I was driving home from Durham, I reflect on how some of my friends have used mantras in their private lives to keep them focussed.

One friend has the aspiration to live to be one hundred, so his mantra is 'Moderation in all things'.

Another friend struggled to prioritise both at home and at work – he called it multi-tasking but struggled to complete anything. He adopted the mantra 'First things first, second things not at all'. He said it helped him to get things done, because he focussed on the important stuff and left the minor things until later.

My friend Gerard Egan, who argued that too often his clients procrastinated instead of getting things done, favoured the mantra 'Now is good'.

I reflect on my mantra. 'Just do it!' Sometimes it works.

Do you have a mantra?

If not, what do you think would help you stay focussed right now?

Some effective mantras:

- Let go to grow
- KISS (keep it simple stupid)
- Delighting Customers
- Work hard play hard
- Look after the pennies and the pounds look after themselves.
- If this was my business what would I do?
- There is no 'I' in Team
- First things first Second things not at all.
- Keep your eyes on the prize

Chapter Thirty-Two
Revolutionary reads

Before travelling on the train from Hull to London, I select a favourite book to read on the journey: *The Practice of Management* by Peter F Drucker.

This was the first ever and possibly the best business book I have ever read. Thinking about it now, there is little wonder that I was mesmerised – it was ground-breaking. I've read it at least five times over the last fifty years, and each time I've been inspired by his wonderful writing. I'm looking forward to enjoying my sixth read.

I gaze out of the window at the fields of wind turbines, pondering on how the view from the train has changed over fifty years. I think about the changing business landscape and the books in my life that have influenced me.

Certainly, the one I have on my table right now, *The Practice of Management*, inspired a generation including me to take a deeper interest in business and management. Published in 1954, it was the first truly management-focussed book, and the first to describe management as a distinct function. Up to this point very few managers knew what they should do. Drucker changed that forever.

I had to wait another twenty years for the next ground-breaking business book to come along. *In Search of Excellence* by Tom Peters and Robert Waterman was published in 1982. They had researched the top performing businesses in the USA at that time to discover what they had done to become the best in their fields. It was a page turner, selling three million copies in the first four years.

They identified eight key factors which these businesses had in common and coined some memorable chapter titles: Delighting Customers; Stick to the Knitting; Productivity through People and so on. These mantras became the core content of many business school and consultancy programmes for the next decade.

How did I benefit from Peters and Waterman's work? I used it extensively in my own consultancy practice. I had discovered it in 1982 on a U.S. business trip to Tucson, Arizona – *In Search of Excellence* was in every bookshop window. I devoured it and brought it back to my number one client, Terry Bramall. He read it and immediately bought twenty copies for his management team.

'We will compete by Delighting Customers!' he proclaimed. It helped them to became industry leaders by delivering outstanding customer service.

Another twenty years went by until the next inspirational book came along.

Good to Great by Jim Collins became a world best seller in 2001. He identified and compared the leading businesses in ten American sectors who were outperforming their competition tenfold! Wells Fargo bank v Bank of America for example.

In his book, Collins identifies ten key things that made a significant difference. Again, I use his work in my consulting practice. For example, the concept of 'Getting the right people on the bus' proved to be a game changer for several of my clients.

So, three books over forty years really helped me in my work. What was it about them that made them ground-breaking?

They captured the business mood of the moment and, incidentally, became worldwide best sellers. They are the only books that I still refer to regularly and have given them to many clients. The findings in all of them are based on extensive research. When you apply their insights they generally work.

Finally, they are all well written and are great page turners.

I had the good fortune to meet Tom Peters and Jim Collins, but to my deep regret I never met Peter Drucker.

I am challenged by my writing coach Deb. 'These books go back years they may make you look off the pace.'

So I went through my library and scoured Google: *Top business books over the past Ten years*. My conclusion is that there have been some other good business books, mainly biographies about global business giants such as, *Steve Jobs by Walter Isaacson, Richard Branson The Virgin Way, and Jack by Jack Welsh*. But in my opinion, these are not great books, that changed the way businesses think and behave.

So Deb, I am happy with my three game changing block busters. Thank you

'*The train is now pulling into King Cross please take all your belongs with you…*' The guard's announcement wakens me from my nostalgic musings.

I carefully tuck the book into my briefcase.

Postscript

Since I wrote this memoir Covid-19 burst on the scene. As a result of the carnage in the business world entrepreneurs need to innovate and rethink their business models to survive and prosper. Tom Peters wrote a good book back in 2009: *Re-imagine! Business excellence in a disruptive age*. It has some good ideas which entrepreneurs may find helpful in these difficult times.

Chapter Thirty-Three

Meetings bloody meetings

I have spent a good portion of my life sitting in meetings that frankly are a waste of everybody's time. No agenda, people pontificating, no action points, little progress on anything.

Meetings for meetings sake.

In 1976 John Cleese tried to help, when his company Video Arts, made an award-winning video called *Meetings Bloody Meetings*. Cleese was always interested in making money (primarily to pay for his many divorce settlements). His business was very successful, providing resources for training programmes.

However, I don't see any evidence that his video '*Meetings Bloody Meetings*' has changed the quality of many meetings I have suffered, since that time.

Take Neville, a client of mine, who recently complained to me:

'Our weekly meetings are hopeless. We go over the same ground every week, with little benefit to the business. They take up half the day. People find them boring and they make up any excuse not to attend.'

'How long have you been holding these meetings?' I ask.

'Oh, for about ten years now.'

'Neville, I give you permission to stop holding these meetings, my friend.'

I reminded Neville that the Prime Minister runs the country on a weekly cabinet meeting that lasts just an hour. That meeting only goes on longer, if there is a national crisis.

However, I did attend one meeting which ticked all the boxes. It was chaired by Geoff Spencer, CEO of DB Shenker.

Geoff's performance management meeting is held every Monday without fail from eleven to twelve noon. Attendance by his senior team is compulsory, no excuses. The office door is locked at eleven sharp and latecomers are not allowed in. Geoff's logic is this:

'We are running a railway business; our trains need to set off and arrive on time. So how can we deliver that, if we can't even attend a fucking meeting on time?'

His meeting lasts for one hour. There are no chairs. People stand by whiteboards where their action plans are displayed with targets, dates and names allocated. They report on their progress; generalisations like 'it's works in progress' are not permitted. They are only permitted to miss a target or deadline twice and then they are sacked or demoted, two strikes and they are out.

'This is brutal, Geoff,' I comment when I attended my first meeting as a collaborator.

'This business is in trouble; we need to be disciplined to sort it, and quick. There is no time to take prisoners.'

I spoke to the people who attended, and they all said it was hard, but necessary. They understood and really appreciated Geoff's tough leadership approach.

I reflected on Geoff's meetings. Clearly, this is not the answer to all meeting situations, but it does have some of the qualities so sorely lacking in many of the meetings I have to attend: strong chair, clear agenda, time bound, factual reporting, attendees taking personal responsibility for delivering actions, listening to colleagues, focus on business enhancing objectives and minimal waffling.

Perhaps this is a recipe for all successful management meetings?

Now how about the Shadow Side of meetings? All those things that people say and do, that rarely get challenged, but can have a big effect on the culture and outcomes of a meeting.

One thing I have learned is not to confuse confidence and competence. Some speak eloquently and as if they have all the answers, gleaned from a 'credible source'. They are rarely challenged. Try asking 'can you please send me a copy of the research you quote,' and watch their reaction….

Another behaviour that often sabotages meetings is 'I'm sure that everybody agrees with me when I say…' No, we fucking don't!

Or the person who always wants to be centre stage and never stops talking, yet offers no new content, overshadowing other quieter members, leading to poor quality outcomes and frustration for all attendees.

Poorly chaired meetings are the cause of much frustration. A chair who does not stick to the agenda or timetable and allows long discussions on priorities like; where to hold the Christmas party at the expense of some important strategic decisions that require attention.

The culture of a business's meetings reflects its culture and how well the business is managed. They set the tone for creating a performance-based culture, where everybody takes personal responsibility for delivering the required results. See *Toolkit 3: Crafting Culture.*

End of sermon.

Chapter Thirty-Four
Aussie Adventures

Most of my research and consulting experiences have been with UK businesses. I am keen to discover whether my material is relevant in other countries and cultures.

In 2000, I received a phone call, out of the blue.

'David, I've left Durham and taken a job as Director of the Small Business Unit in Perth, Australia. Yes, Australia! Do you fancy coming over? I'd love to pick up our collaboration. And by the way, David, it's not all swagmen and kangaroos – Australia's come a long way since Crocodile Dundee and cowboy hats with those dangling corks...'

I interrupted. 'Hello, Tim.'

The call was from Tim Atterton, Director of Curtin University in Perth, Western Australia. I first met Tim at a U.K. marketing conference in 1984, when he was Director of the Small Business Centre at Durham Business School, regarded as one of the best of its kind in Europe. Working together over a number of years, we had together developed several successful programmes for entrepreneurs.

With his usual enthusiasm, Tim rushed on. 'Australia's the fourth richest country in the world and Perth is a bang up-to-date, sophisticated city – it's ranked amongst the Top Ten most 'liveable' cities in the world. You'd love it here!'

I smiled to myself. Tim was always brilliantly persuasive and a great networker, using his skills to engage with people to good effect and to make things happen.

He added, to clinch the deal, 'I'm certain that your no nonsense, straight talking approach will go down a storm with the Aussies!'

'Sounds good, Tim,' I said levelly, but my hand clutching the phone sweated with excitement. 'But who pays for these gigs?'

'No worries, mate' (Aussie-speak already!) 'I've arranged for Qantas to sponsor your flights – business class, of course. Bank West will pay your fees and I've sorted a very nice hotel for you. The University will entertain you at the Test Match at the Wacca and my mate Dave Reid will take us out in his boat to Rotto – Rottnest Island – for a day. All sorted. What do you say?'

This was the chance I had been seeking, an opportunity to test my stuff in a different country… and get paid to do it!

And that's how my Australian adventures began.

The flight to Perth was uneventful, although it seemed to take a bloody week to get there! When I arrived at Perth airport, there was no sign of Tim. Jet lagged and grouchy, I called his mobile.

'No dramas, bananas – you're in Oz now, mate. Chill out. Be with you in a tick.'

'Tim, where the hell are you? I'll give you bloody bananas.'

I shouldn't have been surprised that Tim was late. His networking skills were amazing, but his time management skills were woeful.

He greeted me with a big broad grin 'Brought your sunscreen?'

'Yes – Factor 30. Not taking any chances.'

'Bloody hell. You need total sunblock here or you'll fry! There's a hole in the atmosphere, right over Perth.'

The Broadwater Resort in Como, an apartment hotel, was a great place to stay. Each suite had its own bedroom, lounge and fully fitted kitchen; there was also a top-class restaurant, bar and outdoor swimming pool. Fabulous. Tim had done good.

My first gig was for budding entrepreneurs, men and woman, who flew in from all over Western Australia, piloting their own small light aircraft. They hailed from farms and businesses scattered hundreds of miles across the vast outback. No business suits here: these suntanned guys wore shorts and the inevitable outback boots made by R.M. Williams – and no socks. They were the craziest, funniest and most enthusiastic bunch I have ever worked with. Brilliant.

The focus of the first seminar was 'How entrepreneurs create great small businesses'. We covered a wide range of topics – the importance of personal skills, visioning, spotting opportunities, persistence and positivity. Afterwards I said to Tim, 'They lapped it up as if they'd never heard any of it before!'

He looked at me as if I had landed from another planet. 'They haven't! That's why you're here, mate. In Australia, the Chamber of Commerce is very powerful. It's dominated by the global mining companies who jet in business 'gurus' from the States. They churn out all the corporate MBA guff – most of it completely irrelevant. You, on the other hand, talk their language. You're a first, for most of them.'

So there we were. The purpose of my trip had been to test my material abroad. The Aussies had lapped it up. Tim was reassuring. 'Your approach is completely new and a revelation to them. I told you it would go down well. They loved you.' It seemed that, not only was my stuff relevant to another kind of business culture – it was well received, too. Result.

It wasn't all work, either. Tim's mate Dave hired a boat and he took a gang of us, with the indispensable 'Eski' (short for 'Eskimo': Australian for a beer-filled cool-box), to Rottnest Island. Its name doesn't do it justice. Its beaches are lovely, clean white sand, tropical vegetation and azure blue sea. it's populated by quokkas, a wallaby-like marsupial about the size of a small lamb, and unique to Rottnest. It has been described as the happiest animal on earth and I can understand why. I'd be happy ever after, living on Rottnest Island with them.

The trip out there was on a flat calm, tranquil sea; but we faced ten-foot waves all the way back. I felt ill but got no sympathy – the Aussies just laughed at a Pom's discomfort. (Oh, and on that trip, I was told the definition of Pom: a 'Prisoner of Her Majesty'. It was coined in the 1930s to describe British immigrants arriving on prison ships, with bad skin as wrinkled and leathery as a pom-egranate.)

My next gig was held at the University, hosting two hundred delegates from the great and good of Perth's business community. I needed to get the audience quickly on my side.

'Two hundred years ago we Brits sent your ancestors on prison ships to Australia, to a continent of blue skies, sunshine, lovely beaches, plenty of land and eighty percent of the world's mineral resources. We stayed at home, to enjoy the rain and cold, the lousy British summers and the misery of poverty and rickets.'

The audience went wild, laughing, whistling and applauding. I think I won them over.

Over the two following two weeks, I shared my material and experiences with several groups of entrepreneurs, bankers and academics. It was well received.

I had grown to really like the Aussies. They work to live – not the other way around. It's quite usual to start and finish early most days, collect the kids from school and head straight to the beach. What a lifestyle.

They even taught me how to say 'Australian' properly. Try it. Say 'Stri Len' quickly… See? It works.

One memorable day, I caught the morning 'red eye' to Sydney. I'd been asked by my sponsors, Bank West, to present a workshop to their staff at head office. Sidney is a lovely city – wish I could have stayed longer. Then it was onto Melbourne to give a broadcast interview for a business programme on breakfast TV. Back to Perth on the late-night flight. Phew!

I have some great memories of this trip. Swimming off Manley Beach; visiting the Wacca and the MCG cricket grounds; marvelling at the iconic Sydney Opera House whilst taking one of the ferries across vast Sydney Harbour; and eating Aussie meat pie and peas with a plastic spoon at Harry's Café de Wheels – an iconic pop-up van parked in the Harbour and frequented by celebrities from around the world.

Most of all, I enjoyed mixing with some of the most positive, friendly, happy and hard working people I have ever met.

Tim said, 'When Australia failed to win a medal in the 1956 Olympic games, held in Melbourne, it was such a national embarrassment that the government agreed that it must never happen again!' He described how they redesigned the education system so that any child, above a certain age, who showed promise in any sporting activity, could attend a school that specialised in that sport. Schools invested in specialist coaches to train young people in sports such as cricket, rugby, swimming, athletics and tennis. Now budding swimmers, who had previously received a one-hour lesson a week, had at least one full day's coaching every Saturday.

The results have been staggering and Australia now dominates the world in many of these sports. An additional apparent benefit is the pride they take in their country, communities and all things Australian.

'I've noticed, Tim, that there's hardly any graffiti or litter, anywhere,' I said, thinking of the rubbish strewn streets back home.

He replied with the passion of a new convert. 'That's another bonus. Here, people take pride in keeping their country clean and tidy. This is a culture transformed by sport!'

Of all the places I have visited, Australia is one to which I could happily have emigrated, like Tim. My two week visit flew by and I promised myself that I'd be back, as soon as possible.

Chapter Thirty-Five
A visit to the Outback

I am keen to get back to Australia and renew my acquaintance with my new Aussie 'mates'.

Great minds must think alike because my friend and sponsor, Tim Atterton called me from Perth.

'I'd like to organise some workshops based on your book, *Doing the Business*. And the fact that it's sponsored by Richard Branson will definitely help promote your tour.'

Always a master of the understatement.

I'm thrilled. Another opportunity to test my latest material in another culture – and my chance to head 'down under'. Three weeks later it was sorted.

I'd decided that we could use this second Australian conference to fund a holiday for my wife Ellen and Penny, our daughter. Tim weaved his magic once again and organised the whole trip. He also persuaded a car dealership to loan us a Saab convertible, so that Ellen and Penny could explore parts of Western Australia whilst I strutted my stuff.

This time the main gig was held in the brand new Perth Convention Centre, built to accommodate seven hundred people.

'Last week, David, the international business guru, Tom Peters, performed to an audience of five hundred business people. We've got over six hundred and fifty bookings. You don't get stage fright, do you....?'

This record attendance was entirely down to Tim's brilliant networking – not my fame! However, I was quietly proud to have outgunned one of my heroes, the great Tom Peters.

It started well but then after twenty minutes the lapel microphone sound system went down... We waited ten minutes the audience started getting unsettled, so I had to deliver the whole days session with a handheld microphone like bloody Bruce Forsyth! Thank god it went okay, and we got some excellent reviews by the delegates and the media.

My next audience was a group of high-flying Australian CEOs, members of The Young Presidents Organisation (YPO).

'But,' said Tim, 'there is one thing I forgot to mention, David. They're on a retreat in the wilderness. You'll be driven into the outback, about a four hour trip, and then you'll do your stuff round the campfire that evening. You'll love it. See you tomorrow, when you get back – if you get back.' He grinned at me.

I was speechless. Almost. 'Tim. What the fuck...?'

We drove for hours through bush in the dark with kangaroos and other animals leaping across the road in front of us. My driver just laughed at my terror.

We were met by fifty YPs, Harvard types dressed in pale blue cotton Oxford shirts with button down collars, designer shorts and the obligatory R.M. Williams outback boots – and once again, no socks.

These are serious high-flying entrepreneurs. We sat on logs around a campfire until two in the morning, all of us drinking beer whilst I rattled on about managers not taking business too seriously. Not the most appropriate material for that audience, but Tim had forgotten to brief me fully. It was too late to change my script, so I winged it. I was accompanied by plenty of good-natured barracking and singing. I survived, just.

The following weekend, Ellen, Penny and I drove to the nearby port of Freemantle (Freo) where, in years gone by, the British convict ships had docked after their arduous voyages. It was now a lovely place, full of elegant shops and trendy cafes and bars.

'Your ancestors must have thought they were on holiday when they got here,' I goaded my new Aussie mates.

That afternoon a sea breeze, nicknamed 'the Doctor', swept in from Freo, bringing welcome relief to the cricketers at the Wacca who were suffering in the heat. Tim suggested that we visit Cottesloe Beach.

'It's the most beautiful in the region,' he said. 'Great for swimming but – let me give you a tip – if no-one's in the water, don't go in!' He winked. 'Great White sharks or box jelly fish, mate. Don't want to worry you, but last week a Great White killed a surfer, just ten metres from the shore.'

Cottesloe was a superb beach, buzzing with swimmers and surfers – but we gave the sea a miss....just in case.

It occurs to me that I haven't written much about business or management in these recollections of Australia. My feelings are all about the people and the places I visited. That's how Australia got to me and why I love the place so much.

Now back to business. My book entitled 'Doing the Business', published in 2002 is a series of 37 original 'Toolkits' designed to provide managers with some structure (I call them 'roadmaps') to help them, for example, to make decisions, motivate staff and cut costs.

I introduced the toolkits to several audiences in Perth, Melbourne and Sydney. The response was generally enthusiastic, with many requests for copies of the book.

I had asked myself the question: Do I need to change any of the content to fit Australian audiences? The response was a clear NO. A satisfying outcome.

Chapter Thirty-Six

Oz – the finale

I **was dreading the call.**

'David, I've got some great gigs lined up for you in Oz this summer!'

I took a deep breath. 'Thanks, Tim but having been there for the past two years, I can't really afford the time, I am really busy.'

'Come on, David. I've put together a great itinerary for you, mate. You'll love it.'

'I appreciate it, Tim, I really do. But I can't make the trip this year, I'm afraid – maybe in another year or two.'

'Okay, if it's money, I'll get you more fees. What else would persuade you to come?'

I really liked Tim and was grateful for all he had done for me – but he could be persistent. I thought for a moment. What could I ask for that he couldn't possibly deliver?

'Okay Tim, how about you make me a Professor of Curtin Business School?'

There was a pause. 'Leave it with me,' he replied.

Two days later I get another call from Tim. 'How quickly can you get your CV together? I'll send you the format for a Professorship application.

Oh, and I am sure Professors Allan Gibb and Ted Fuller will act as your referees.'*

I was stunned and rather uncertain whether to be delighted or dismayed by Tim's call – but obediently I filled in the form. As promised, Allan and Ted provided me with very kind references and, within a month, I received a letter from the Dean of Perth Business School.

'Congratulations, Professor Hall, welcome to the Curtin team.'

I'd been outmanoeuvred by my friend Tim! And, of course, I was elated with the professorship. My only regret was that I couldn't share the excitement with Mum, who had died the previous year.

Furthermore, I realised that this was a great opportunity to test more of my material, particularly the Growth Programme, that Tim and I had developed together at Durham Business School, this was geared specifically for mid-sized owner-managed businesses. I couldn't wait to get back out there.

Tim had booked me a flight with Malaysian Airlines. I noticed that each stewardess addressed every passenger by name, apparently from memory. An admirable skill and a great personal touch. How did they do it?

'We're trained to memorise each passenger's name from on our list. Our customers really appreciate it. Our training is envied by the other Asian airlines, so now we train them too.'

Very impressive. I settled back to contemplate my itinerary.

I had a long trip ahead of me – three weeks in total, visiting Perth, Sydney and Melbourne. The flight from Perth to Sydney is 1022 miles and it crosses two time zones. Sydney to Melbourne is 221 miles. Another interesting stat is that Perth is the city furthest away from any other city in the world.

Everything went to schedule but this time, to my surprise, I felt a touch of homesickness. I loved meeting the people but found I had already seen many of the sights. The hotels were great, but dining solo was lonely, the nights even more so. I wished Ellen was sharing the trip with me, like last time.

The trip's finale, back at Curtin University, was the programme of Growth Workshops for entrepreneurs which Tim and I had developed fifteen years earlier. Thousands of entrepreneurs have attended the Growth Programme over the years. These sessions were based on my book, *Hallmarks for Successful Business Development,* * and were inspired by our research into how small businesses grow successfully.

As before, the participants are keen to get very involved and learn. I asked Tim if they were always as enthusiastic.

'Remember that, before you came along, they've never had material that is relevant to their world, only big company stuff. You're a breath of air.'

'Christ, Tim! We should have charged them more!'

My trip was over. Would I ever come back? I really hoped so. I love the people and that they seem to value my work.

I got to the airport early for the flight home. Four hours too early, in fact. Couldn't wait to board flight ML 346 and get back to the rain, cold, poverty and misery of the lovely UK.

Twelve months later I got a call from Tim. He was no longer Director of the Curtin University Small Business Centre. Apparently, the University bureaucracy didn't like the fact he was spending 'too much time doing private consultancy work'. I was astonished.

In typical public sector, bureaucratic fashion, the university had ignored the fact that Tim was responsible for creating one of the most successful entrepreneurial programmes in Western Australia. He had lifted the Curtin Small Business Centre into the premier league of business schools and attracted more support from entrepreneurs and financial sponsors in the last ten years than the Centre had enjoyed in the previous fifty.

Since his departure from Curtin over the past ten years Tim has helped Murdoch University in Perth (a Curtin competitor) and Duke CE in the USA to establish the Financial Dynamics programmes that he had originally developed at Durham and latterly at Curtin. He has worked in fifty countries around the world, including Kenya, South Africa and Dubai, helping government agencies and banks to establish enterprise support systems and programmes.

Tim was very good to me and his work around the world deserves great respect. I feel lucky to have played a part in some of his enterprises.

Postscript

2020. It's now sixteen years since Tim and I worked together in Australia. I have missed working with him. I have now added a trip to Perth to my bucket list.

I decided to send my three Oz memoirs to Tim so that he could correct any errors in my recollection of our adventures together. Here is part of his reply:

'Thanks for the blogs, which I really enjoyed reading. They brought back many, many very fond and happy memories. Your Hallmarks material went down a storm with the Aussies and your concerns about the relevance to a different culture has been proved unfounded. The respect and admiration are mutual – what the Kiwis call "bro love"… Travel safe, David, and I will be the person at the front of the Reception Committee queue waiting at Perth Airport when you engineer a trip back to OZ.'

*The Hallmarks for Business Development 1992, Management Books 2000

*Both Allan Gibb (sadly deceased in 2020) and Ted Fuller have international reputations as leaders in the field of enterprise and entrepreneurship.

Chapter Thirty-Seven

Business Psychobabble

I wrote this memoir to celebrate taking entrepreneurship and management seriously, but we don't do ourselves any favours in business, by using meaningless management metaphors (MMMs) that annoy people. This undermines our credibility. My friend calls it corporate wank speak (CWS).

People use these phrases to make the obvious and straightforward sound cerebral and exciting.

Here is my CWS dictionary:

'Low hanging fruit'	Easy
'Bring you're A game'	Be prepared
'Light a fire under them'	Motivate
'Tear down the silos'	Remove barriers
'Give 110%'	Do your best
'Take it to the next level'	Improve
'Bite the bullet'	Decide
'Run it up the flagpole'	Test it
'Think outside the box'	Innovate
'Let's socialise this'	Talk to people
'I'm Stacked'	Busy

'Let's not boil the ocean'	Let's give up
'Move the needle'	Improve

That's enough bollocks for now.

Chapter Thirty-Eight

Taking Management Seriously

At **times it makes** me mad that, in my role as a consultant, I come across owners or leaders of businesses who believe they are God's gift to management, when in fact they are fucking useless.

You could argue that I make my living helping them sort out their businesses, so therefore without these people I might, in my mother's words, 'get a proper job'.

A slight digression here. Mum once came to a conference at which I was speaking. I was quite excited, knowing that she was in the audience, and gave it my best shot. Afterwards she said, 'you get paid for doing that?'

So, why does having to deal with arrogant clients make me so cross?

Two reasons. Firstly, a lot of people depend on them to do a good job: employees and their families, customers, suppliers and investors. Managing is not easy, it requires skill, judgment, persistence and the right mindset. Now here's the thing:

Management is the only profession that you get promoted into because you are good at something else, and for which little preparation is thought necessary.

There is no other profession like it.

Typically for example, the top salesperson gets promoted to sales manager, stops selling and tries to manage other salespeople. Often, they fail miserably, but also their business loses the sales they previously delivered. A double whammy.

It's not the sales managers fault, let's get that straight. It's the system that promotes them into a management role, whether they have the ability or not, and then fails to train or prepare them for it. They don't really know what to do, so they look around at other managers or to their own boss for clues, but often those guys are just as hopeless and helpless.

Management is a profession into which people are ordained, not trained. This is very sad for all concerned, don't you think?

The second reason it makes me angry is that many of these 'managers', once promoted, become smug and arrogant. Their arrogance is only exceeded by their ignorance. Nobody really wants to work for them, it's becomes 'just a job'; doing the minimum to survive, rather than treating it as a responsibility. People tend to leave poor managers, not the organisations they work for.

These ingredients combine to produce results beneath expectations, or even business failure.

So, what's the answer?

Promote people into management roles because they have the potential and qualities to manage – and then train them for the role.

Now the best part of my job is when I meet a great manager and leader. I have worked with some good managers but very few great ones. On the 17 March 2015 I had the good fortune to meet one example of this rare breed. Geoff Spencer was CEO of the German-owned, global railway giant, DB Schenker. I had been asked to coach him by a friend because he was 'an awkward bugger and so are you.'

As soon as I met Geoff, I recognised him from when I did some work in his previous business EWS Railway. I told him exactly why my friend had put us both together. 'She said Geoff is an awkward bugger and so are you!'

We both roared with laughter. It was one of those rare encounters when you just know you will get on well together.

Perhaps it helped that we both shared similar stories, starting at the bottom of the ladder and climbing our way up. Geoff was similar in build to me – both of us needed to lose weight and to get fit. We both enjoyed a beer, having a laugh and not taking ourselves too seriously. A bond was forged, and we agreed to work together.

I was looking forward to working with Geoff Spencer. I told him he must be brutally honest with me and that whatever we discussed stayed in the room. Normal coaching contracting stuff.

He replied, 'If you're not bloody honest with me, you're out!'

This guy's life story was amazing. He summarised his career with the railway.

'I was a Huddersfield lad with no qualifications. I started my working life as a trainee train driver and loved it. Then I got promoted through the ranks, because I made sure I over-delivered and exceeded expectations in every job I did. When we met, 20 years ago David, I was a middle manager. After that I got promoted every three years, eventually moving to Germany as Head of Resource Management of the European division. In 2014 I was appointed CEO of the UK business.' He shrugged modestly, grinned at me and went on.

'By then, I'd done just about every job in the business, and nobody could pull the wool over my eyes. I knew where all the skeletons were hidden and what we needed to do to take the business forward.'

'Wow!' I responded, 'great story, Geoff. So what can I do to help?'

'Well, first let me tell you about our business challenges. Ask me any questions you like and let's see how we go.'

We spend a few hours talking together and quickly it became clear that this guy was 'on it'. He had succeeded in doing many of the things that are the hallmarks of a great manager. In my experience he is unique.

He identified one area he needed to tackle with his team, to develop a long-term plan. I agreed to help him. As I worked with Geoff and his board, I watched how he operated as the leader; he was assertive and demanding, setting the bar high for the business and the individuals. He wanted decision-making based on good analysis, challenged negativity, allocated individuals to tasks and injected energy and pace into actions to overcome complacency. It was a masterclass in leadership and team building. See *Toolkit 8: Lessons from Entrepreneurial Leaders*

I asked him how he had developed his leadership style. He thought for a moment.

'I am a good learner, I think, and I've always tried to work with people who get things done. I work hard at communicating constantly with my team. I am brutally honest which I think they value. Treating people with dignity and respect is a priority as is having total integrity. I don't read books or attend training courses, but I ensure I get people alongside me who can help me. That's it, really.'

I concluded that this guy was a one-in-a-million natural, a gifted manager who used his intuition and simply tried to do the right thing for customers, colleagues and the business, He stood up and started gently pacing up and down his office.

But most of all, he was a nice guy, liked by people who therefore wanted to follow him.

It is a quality called LEADERSHIP.

Chapter Thirty-Nine

Gastro Pubs

I'm visiting a client located just north of London who has asked
me to help him improve the performance of his chain of gastropubs.
It's been a while since I worked with someone in the food business, so I
am looking forward to it. I arrive at his home for our first meeting. It's a
mansion! The largest, most palatial house I've ever been in.

The owner (let's call him George) is a fit looking individual, tanned and
well dressed. He'd made his money – several hundred million pounds –
as a member of a well-known family business and had benefited when it
was sold for several billions in 2005.

He used some of the money to invest in several businesses, none of which,
I discovered later, were profitable. This pub chain was one of them.

'We've invested in six gastropubs in the past three years and have
completely refurbished them – no expense spared!' he proudly informed
me. 'I've arranged to take you to our local one today.'

Off we went in his bright red Aston Martin. He was right, the pub had
been fitted out expensively, with natural light oak doors, tables and bar
fittings. It was magnificent.

'Fancy a sandwich, David?'

The waitress who takes our order looks about sixteen; the others look no
older.

'What's the special today?' I ask her.

'Um, sorry, don't know.'

'Well, what would you recommend?'

'Don't know. This is only my second day,' she says lamely.

Does anyone know?

It gets worse, I order a beef sandwich on brown, a ham sandwich on white arrives.

George looks embarrassed and livid. 'Sorry. It's a real struggle to get decent staff and we can't seem to keep the good ones.'

Why do restaurants invest millions in bricks and mortar, then hire untrained staff and pay them peanuts, is a mystery to me. The consequence is the service is terrible, and the diners don't come back. It's not the staff's fault: they do their best, but are usually untrained, underpaid, under-managed, unmotivated. It's 'just a job' to them.

And it gets worse. They can't find decent chefs for what they are prepared to pay, so they hire almost anyone who comes through the door. The new chef quickly gets fed up with the hours and workload and leaves. The cycle starts all over again. The net result is the food standard is variable at best and the service is poor. No wonder so many restaurants and pubs fail.

'Can you help, David?' George asks. After investing millions in the business, he wants a return on his investment. To make a profit.

I look around me. If he was serious about the business, he should reduce the spend on fancy décor, and hire professional staff, paying them properly. In fact, he seems to have applied the culture from his large corporate business: recruit unskilled staff, work them hard and pay them as little as you can get away with. This mindset will be difficult to change, as it had helped create his success in the past.

Nevertheless, I am intrigued so, against my better judgement, I decided to give it a go.

I come back a week later. Whenever I start a new project, I am always full of anticipation and a degree of confidence that I can sort out the problems. It's always exciting, not knowing what you are going to find.

My initial approach to any project is to ask questions to try and get to the bottom of the client's problems and sort the causes from the effects. Clients always know much more about their business than I do, but they are often too close and can't see the wood for the trees.

They rarely have a clear process by which to identify and sort their issues. I work closely with the client to help them identify and sort out their problems. See *Toolkit 1: Working ON the Business.*

So, I visit one of George's gastropubs the following week to meet the operational manager for the group. Let's call him Ted to spare his blushes.

Ted is a rotund, ruddy faced, enthusiastic, individual who had previously run his own successful business for several years. He is enthusiastic and seems 'on it'. I quickly decide that I like him and want to help him.

'Our problem is that we don't have enough sales or profits,' Ted informs me.

'Okay, so let's start at the beginning, with sales,' I suggest.

After a couple of hours of probing questions, we agree that, before investing in more marketing, it would be useful to review the current quality of both food and service. If they are not right, then creating more customers is likely to do more harm. They won't come back and worse, they'll tell at least five friends about their poor experience. Disaster.

'What's your product offer like?' I ask Ted. 'Be brutally honest – what do you really think?'

He confirms that getting and keeping good staff is the key problem. I make some suggestions and we agree to meet again the following week.

A few days later I am back.

'So, Ted, have you had any thoughts since our last meeting about keeping chefs and training and keeping your waiting staff?'

Ted nods enthusiastically. 'Yes, having spoken to the chefs, the problem seems to be the hours we expect them to work. I'm in the process of changing their rotas to reduce them, and to ask the other chefs to step up and share the workload.'

'How was that idea received?'

'Bloody brilliant! They loved it! It will cost us a bit more to pay their team, but I told the boss we need to do it if we are to get consistency into our offer. The other benefit is that they'll all be more engaged and committed to our business.'

'And the waiting staff?'

'I liked your idea of creating a virtual training academy for people looking for a waiting position. We can build a database of students and others, who we train in our ways, so when we need them, we can call on them, confident they are well trained. It's a potential win – win for all.'

'Ted, you are a delight to work with because you get on and do stuff.'

This is a welcome change from clients who proffer lame excuses for doing fuck all.

'Next, shall we have a go at improving the profits? Start with the principle that the easiest way to make money is to stop losing it. The bulk of the costs are staff and raw materials.'

'I suggest we look at material costs,' says Ted, screwing up his face as if he knows what we are about to discover.

We start with the meat supplier, a large national company. 'They deliver top quality products and supply all the top restaurants,' says Ted with his natural enthusiasm. I casually ask him how often he meets with the supplier. 'Oh, he drops in every two or three months in his helicopter.' I raise an eyebrow. 'Not the local butcher, then... I suggest you get quotes from other suppliers, Ted.'

Over the next three hours we find several ways to reduce costs and improve profits: the chefs butcher steaks from full carcases and the weights varied significantly from 7oz to 12 oz for an 8oz fillet steak on the menu. This inconsistency is costly for the business.

They also bake their own bread at great expense. There's an award-winning bakery up the road who could match the quality at half the cost.

Chefs spend hours making their own stocks, Michelin-starred chef Heston Blumenthal purchases his from a lady in Leeds. If it's good enough for Heston, Ted….

Chefs could purchase individual ingredients from their favourite supplier at any time, at any cost….

We discussed creating a central buying system to take advantage of the scale opportunities from having six outlets. Ted is taking it all on board.

All in all, it seems to me that the business is throwing money out of the window, so later I confront the owner, George.

'You behave like a high end three-star Michelin operation with all the attendant costs. You are, in fact, running gastropubs with an average price mark of £20 per head, not two hundred. No wonder you're losing money – your costs are out of control. You need to decide if this is an ego business or whether you want to make a profit. I believe that Ted can sort it if you let him get on with it.'

'Okay. Well, thank you for your help,' replied George,' looking unconvinced, 'I am sure we'll be calling on you again in the future.'

I can't help feeling that, in the end, Ted will have little say in the matter. I won't be surprised if he leaves. Pity, because I like him, and he personally gets it.

Working collaboratively takes two to tango with me providing a process to follow and adding the experiences of others to illustrate and inspire. The internal person (Ted) then applies it to their business. Ted took to my approach like a duck to water. Unfortunately, his boss George didn't get it. Bosses are either an asset or a liability in the process. George was a bloody liability.

Postscript

Ted calls me three months later. He has fallen out with George and left the business.

Chapter Forty

Tough Love

I was asked two questions by my audience of entrepreneurs and local authority managers, at the annual 'Bizweek' conference at the Bridlington Spa.

'How do leaders get the best out of their people? And are the best leaders warm and cuddly or are they hard-nosed and demanding?'

I had been thinking about this issue for some time. I replied, 'Do you want the short or long answer?' Polite laughter.

'Perhaps we should start with a different question: what do followers (forgive the term) want from their leaders? Research suggests they want three key qualities: honesty – "tell me as it is even if it's bad news"; inspiration – "inspire me to give my best"; and competence – "deliver what say you will". So, how many of you get that from your business or political leaders right now?'

Half a dozen hands shoot up, then slowly three or four more hands are raised.

'Looking around, it seems that, out of two hundred people, only five percent of you guys are getting what you want from your leaders. How do you feel about that?'

A few shaking heads, audible moans and groans.

'Those of you here who are leaders, how many of you believe and hope that you give your people what they want?'

One hundred hands are raised. Interesting. I move on, warming to my subject.

'Now, what do leaders require from their followers? The evidence is they want them to view their work as a responsibility and to go the extra mile, rather than treating it as "just a job", delivering the minimum to get by, watching the clock for home time. So how many of your people take responsibility for producing results beyond your expectations?'

A smattering of hands.

I push on. 'So how do effective leaders get the results they want? Well, one approach is to treat people with respect, get to know them well as individuals and really look after them. A respect agenda helps to win commitment. The focus is on harmony and keeping people happy. This might be called the *Love* approach and normally produces good outcomes. However some leaders go too far, creating a culture like a happy farm. Difficulties arise when individuals don't respond or choose to take advantage.'

'What about bosses who use the stick approach, being really hard on people?' asks a woman at the front.

'This is called the *Tough* approach. It might work in the short term, but people don't usually respond well to threats and they may leave the business. Would you manage your people in this way?' She shakes her head.

'What about bullying people?' she asks

'Do you believe bullying people is the right thing to do?' I ask. 'If you have ever worked for a bully you would know it's horrible. it's not right morally and it does not get results in the long term.

'I had a boss who bullied me. He hated the fact the business owner took a shine to me looked after me when I was just starting out. One day I was so fed up with him I turned on him, put on my stern voice and said "I really would prefer if you did not speak to me like that again." He was really taken aback and by some miracle it worked. It was only later I discovered that being assertive and speaking confidently can work.

'Let's turn back to the evidence. Effective leaders combine the best features of the two approaches and practise what we might call *Tough Love*. They treat people with respect, look after them and reward them well – the *Love* element. But they also performance-manage, set clear goals, coach them and provide honest, constructive feedback. People that do not respond positively after training, support, appropriate feedback and warnings are expendable. The *Tough* side.'

I ask the audience, 'How many of you practice Tough Love?'

A young man in the front row raises his hand. 'I like the concept. Sometimes, being the good guy has definitely backfired.'

'Okay,' I respond, 'so step one is to recognise that performance could improve if you practise Tough Love.' He nods and I wind up the session.

According Jim Collins in his bestselling book, 'Good to Great', research shows that great businesses are no better at recruiting great people, but they deal with poor performance much more quickly and effectively than the merely good ones.

The key to Tough love is getting the balance right. Knowing when to put your arm round people and when to challenge them. In my experience, this is a rare leadership skill.

Here are some things to try.

Find leaders who are good at Tough Love and ask them for their recipe for success. Effective people are usually delighted to be asked for their advice.

Get yourself a personal coach to help you develop your skills and confidence.

If you learn by reading, there are number of good books on the subject. Search Google/Amazon.

Finally, there are usually many people and their families, depending on your poor performer getting it right, and on you for sorting them out. Your job as a manager is to ensure that they don't ruin the business.

The benefits of practising Tough Love are a potential significant increase in people, teams and organisations being more successful for the benefit of all.

Chapter Forty-One

'Helping' a CEO

Many people working in business training get really hung up about how their role is described: consultant, counsellor, mentor, facilitator, coach, advisor and so on. I am as just bad. Usually I label myself 'consultant'. If I want to be less flash, I'm a 'facilitator'. I'm told that the pragmatic Scandinavians have one word for it all: helping. I like it, so from now on, I am a helper.

I have been asked by a colleague if I might be interested in helping a CEO.

Here's the thing: I like working with CEOs. They are usually lonely because they feel they can't talk about difficult issues to their colleagues. As a result they often have interesting challenges to sort out. Oh, and another thing, they are generally not price sensitive.

I arranged to meet the UK CEO of a large UK food business, based in Scotland. Let's call him Mike Smith. He turns out to be a straight-talking Yorkshireman and he looks very familiar. In his early fifties, 17 stone and ruddy faced, he has the strain of trying to sort out the business etched on his face.

We shake hands. 'I think we've met before, Mike,' I say. 'Weren't you a cheeky young, thrusting manager I met back in the mid-nineties?'

'Yeah, that was me! And you were that bloody annoying middle-aged consultant bloke, brought in by our CEO,' he said with a mischievous grin.

We talk and laugh and talk some more, two hours pass in a flash, we agree to work together. I must admit, during the following months we spend a lot of time during my helping sessions just laughing together.

Mike had inherited several difficult problems when he took the job. Their two main markets: frozen ready meals and fresh pasta for some supermarkets were both in decline. Over several months we work through a new strategy, identifying and focussing on his three key priorities: change his top team, halt the decline in sales and improve margins.

It sounds straightforward now, but it was hard work for him, dragging his team through the necessary culture changes to get the business into a much stronger position.

Mike is a joy to work with because he has an open mind, is low on ego, happy to try new ideas and a good leader. Together we forged a new strategy for his business using the Egan models, which he really took to. He created a new definition of his businesses scope and a vision of where he wanted to take the business in 5 years' time. See *Toolkit 10: Redoing Your Strategy to Revitalise Your Business.*

It's very satisfying working with a client who gets it. We moved things forward at a pace and I left him much happier with his business than when we started the project.

Six months later I get a call from Mike out of the blue. He looks ghastly when I turn up at his office, white faced with bags under his eyes. He looks like he hasn't slept for a week. I fear the worst.

He takes a deep breath, looks down and sighs. After what seems like an age he says quietly,

'When Dad died, he left me a personal letter with an instruction not to open it until after he died. I have not opened it in five years because I became paranoid about what it might contain.' He wipes his eyes and looks up at me. 'By the way, I have told no one about this, not even my family.'

This is clearly a difficult issue for Mike, and I feel privileged that he confides in me. After several tearful discussions he decided to open his father's letter which read: 'Mike you were adopted by us at birth and we brought you up as step-parents. Sorry, son. We loved you as our own, but I needed to find a way to tell you.'

He was totally and utterly devastated by this news. He wasn't who he had thought he was for fifty years! Can you begin to imagine his shock? Unbelievable.

I wiped my eyes!

After several more difficult discussions, he eventually decided to try to find out who his real parents were and to discover his real name. This was a tough decision which he anguished over for several weeks.

'I need to visit the local authority and to find out what the process is to discover my real parents.'

Several weeks later after he had made several frustrated telephone calls and visits, he nearly gave up in despair. But then he got in touch with me and asked me to visit him.

He stood up, as I entered his office and started pacing up and down.

'The Local authority people called me and told me they had discovered who my parents where. Apparently, they were two students at Belfast University, she accidently got pregnant, they couldn't keep me so put me up for adoption. David, this whole affair has been incredibly stressful, as you have witnessed but, in the end, I am glad I eventually discovered my real identity.'

'How do you feel now, Mike?'

He sat down and said quietly:

'OK thanks, I have decided that I am happy to keep the name given to me by my loving step-parents and do not feel the need to chase down my original parents.'

He now appeared calm and in control as if he had begun to work his way through this traumatic episode.

I reflected on what I would do in these circumstances, honest truth, I am not sure.

This was the most traumatic Helping experience I have ever had. I almost feel I need counselling myself! But I am truly glad I could help Mike through his nightmare.

Having helped Mike with his historical issue, we moved on to helping him with his future.

Mike was frustrated with the way the corporate business treated him, so he wanted to retire early and pursue other interests. We worked on this together as he found this another difficult decision. 'I have been in food since I was 15, it's in my blood.'

We talked through his options over several weeks and he eventually decided to retire in late 2015.

Mike was a good effective CEO. He is also a good man. He ticked all the boxes had a good strategy, got the right people on his team, customers liked and trusted him, a tough but caring leader that inspired his people. He was one of best CEOs I have ever worked with in forty years.

How many CEOs do you know that ticks all these boxes?

I truly felt that I had learnt more from him and I should be paying him. I told him so.

'No, you are the one person who is brutally honest with me and you always get the balance right between supporting me and challenging me when I need to do something. You helped me through the most difficult decisions I will ever have to take. But you are still a bloody annoying consultant!'

We shake hands and I leave.

We have remained good friends since.

Chapter Forty-Two

Growing the topline

A client, a technology services business in the North West, wanted to improve its sales. They provide telecom and internet services to customers who wanted to outsource these activities.

I met the business owner, Roger, at a business conference in Bridlington. He came up to me and said that I had been recommended by a former client, Geoff Spencer. Roger looked tired and gaunt, as if he has the world's problems on his shoulders.

He told me, 'We are not getting our share of business, in a market that is growing fast. We need to get our act together or we will miss the boat. Can you help me?'

'Well, what do you think the problem is?' I asked.

'Not sure, it's definitely sales but I am too close to it and need an objective unbiased view.'

'Okay Roger, erm can I think about it for a day or so?'

I wanted to check Roger out with Geoff, so I was buying some time to enable me to talk to Geoff.

'Yea, he is a good guy David, I wouldn't put you in touch with nutters!'

Unexpectedly Roger called the next day,

'Have you made your mind up yet...'

'Okay here is how I work. We need to find an internal person who I can work with. It's the most cost-effective way for you. They need to understand your sales process, be smart, keen, hardworking, and open minded.'

'Right that's John, he ticks all those boxes,' Roger has cheered up a bit now.

John was selected as the leader of a project to work with me to boost sales. He was a sales manager. I initially thought he was a bit cocky and pushy, with his fancy Gucci shoes and Rod Stewart hair style – a fast talking salesman. I gave John a copy of my *Toolkit 1: Working ON the Business* to help him.

John told me 'I initially reviewed the existing sales performance indicators. I discovered that three members of the sales team were producing 80% of the sales. We have seven sales people. The sales director brings in most of the larger contracts. We have 6 products, but most customers only buy 2 products.'

I discussed my findings with Roger, and he assured me that we had an opportunity to increases sales. I told him I think I need to find out how the successful salespeople do it, including the sales director.

In order try to help, I introduced John to a client, whose sales generation system was one the best I have seen.

Afterwards I asked him what he learnt from that experience.

'David, their salespeople were amazing. They ask lots of questions of their customers and then set out to try to solve any problems they have unearthed. They take a genuine interest in helping their customers to succeed. This is nothing like the transactional selling we do; they are partnering with their customers for the long run.'

'How do they train their people to perform at that level John?'

'Well here's the thing, they have found that selection beats training 10-fold. They discovered that their best sales people all have similar profiles on the psychometric test they use as part of the recruitment process. The key scores are achievement focus, drive, sociable and ambitious. Other factors such as intelligence, detail conscious or embracing change appear irrelevant in relation to high performance.'

John was clearly impressed 'I think we really should think about assessing our sales people in a similar way.'

John also learned that the business I had introduced him to, had a very effective sales generation system.

'Instead of managing sales by looking at last month's results, they have a system which looks forward and tells them how many customer visits they need to make each month. They know what their conversion rate should be and their average order size. it's brilliant. It gives them certainty and their boss told me he sleeps much easier in his bed, knowing that they will deliver the sales, he requires.'

'When I told Roger he told me, I like that idea John let's do it.'

'Not yet John, we need to do more work on your customer service performance, no point in boosting our sales if you let your customers down, that could create more problems.'

A review of the customer service records revealed a real problem with their communication with customers. See *Toolkit 6: Getting Customer Service Right.*

'It's not that you're late it's that you never let us know you are going to be late; sums up the number one service problem that you clearly need to address.' I told John.

John and I talked about establishing some simple ground rules to help manage the communications problem. I came up with an idea that I had previously introduced into a legal practice, who had similar communication problems.

The rule was that every customer gets their call returned the same day, no exceptions. We found that a telephone call saying 'X is in court today, but he will call before 9am tomorrow' solved the issue for 90% of their clients.

John introduced the rule of a returning all customer calls the same day. He got Roger to go around the offices, driving people crazy by asking them, 'Have you returned all your calls today?'

'Typically I've found it takes around twelve months before returning calls the same day just becomes the norm.'

Once the service problem had been addressed, John got permission from Roger, to introduce selection testing as part of the recruitment process, starting with the existing team. The psychometric test was evaluated against their performance. Three of whom were clearly not cut out for selling in the new partnering manner so were reallocated to jobs with less direct customer contact.

Testing became a non-negotiable step in the recruitment process for the sales team. Roger told me with a big smile on his face, 'The sales team changes took us six months to complete; sales are now increasing faster than any time in the past five years.'

What lessons had John learnt from the project?

'Firstly you need a process to guide you, your Toolkit was helpful. It important to get the facts to really understand the issue you are trying to address. Fortunately, we had good KPI's which helped me pinpoint where we needed to improve.'

There are always some businesses who have sorted the problem you face; you just need to find them and politely ask for their help. I found most are very happy to show off how good they are!

You need to get the right people on the bus, doing the right things, particularly in sales roles.

You need a system to manage sales activity looking forward not backward that's like driving a car looking through the rear-view mirror.

Finally you can change the culture, but it needs simple rules that people understand and a boss who champions it, until it's becomes 'just the way we do things here'.

The business significantly increased its market share over the next three years. I was wrong about John he turned out to be a real find. I suggested to Roger, that he should treat John to a new pair of designer shoes as a well-earned reward.

'That's a good idea, he said, I don't want to lose him to a competitor.'

Another happy customer.

Chapter Forty-Three
For Entrepreneurs Only (FEO)

I **met a potential new** client, Dave Kilburn today. David was made redundant at 50. Twenty five years later his business MKM Building Supplies, is the largest independent builders' merchant in the UK. It's a fabulous entrepreneurial success story.

We met in our local pub, The Hotham Arms, to talk about his business.

David wears a smart suit and looks well groomed.

But before I can ask him about his business, he launches into a passionate discourse.

'David, I'm really concerned about our regional economy. Local unemployment is amongst the worst in the country and kids leaving school have little chance of getting a job. It's desperate.'

He grimaces.

'So, what are local entrepreneurs like you doing about it?' I ask.

'Believe me I have been involved with every agency you can think off: Chamber of Commerce, Institute of Directors, local authority Task Forces. They've achieved nothing. Ticking boxes, going through the motions but achieving little.'

'Okay, so let's actually try to do something about it, do other business people in Hull share your frustrations?'

'Yes, we've all tried working with different organisations over the years, but we never got very far.'

'Right, so why don't we get these business contacts of yours together and see if we can do something about it ourselves?'

He quickly changed from doom and gloom to becoming exited, 'We could hold a dinner here at the Hotham Arms. I will invite my contact's and we could discuss it.'

'Right that's a plan then.'

He must be happier, he picked he the drinks bill.

Two weeks later twelve business people David invited, turn up for dinner – a positive sign.

David launches into his passionate speech about his concerns: unemployment and the dire local economy.

'Yeah, I have sat on every advisory board in the region,' says Paul Sewell. 'Waste of bloody time.'

'I'm interested in going into schools, to try to inspire the next generation,' says Tom Martin enthusiastically.

It is immediately clear that everybody in the room shares the same frustrations with the lamentable performance of the agencies in the region, who have the remit to deliver economic growth. A clear consensus emerges that we should do something about it.

The first action agreed, is to organise another dinner, each attendee offering to invite one additional business person to create a larger group.

I offer to put together some ideas.

We have lift-off.

After six months the group has forty business members. My PA Lynn is doing the admin. I suggested a name: For Entrepreneurs Only. Members feel that they want this initiative to be just for entrepreneurs and not large corporate businesses, public sector, or organisations that might be tempted to join the group to sell their services.

'We don't want the energy vampires involved. Let's keep it pure,' is the general consensus.

'But we might be accused of being elitist,' somebody suggests meekly.

'Yes, and we are. It is for entrepreneurs only, end of.'

I helped to facilitate the design of a five-year strategy with the overall mission of; *'Helping the local economy by creating wealth and jobs.'*

This became the mantra to guide our key decisions.

Three teams are formed: one helping start-ups, another helping existing businesses to grow and the third to focus on inspiring school kids to become entrepreneurs. A volunteer leader is appointed for each team.

To fund our activities, it's decided that members would pay an annual subscription based on their turnover. The group are clear that they don't want to 'take the queens shilling', or we would be ticking boxes again for other public sector organisations.

Events are organised and run by members who all give their time generously.

This is unique and getting exciting.

It amazes me that busy business people, pay to join and then give their time to support other businesses. It confirms my belief that true entrepreneurs seek to do the right thing; give and take, whereas racketeers are just takers.

I can't think of any other organisation that enjoys this level of commitment to helping other businesses.

Ten years later FEO has 180 active entrepreneurial members. Since 2011 we have helped: 400 people start their own business, with a high success rate; run Masterclasses in eighty schools for over two thousand children, helped 150 existing businesses to grow. Members have added 2300 jobs to the region, 180 business people have been mentored by members. Not bad! I am very proud of the work FEO members have delivered.

It has not been all been plain sailing. FEO is a voluntary organisation; members gravitate to what they are comfortable with and enjoy doing. Some prefer going into schools and running enterprise masterclasses, whilst others like helping business start-ups. My passion is to help helping existing businesses to grow and create new jobs.

Cards on the table, here is my problem.

FEO's strategy, which I helped craft, is to help the local economy by creating wealth and jobs. The evidence is that helping existing businesses to grow is by far the best way to achieve that goal. However, the bulk of FEO's scarce resources and members time is spent with schools and start-ups. It's clear to me we needed to focus on the short-term priority, which means helping existing business to grow and create new jobs. The board disagreed.

Maybe I should have tried harder to help FEO refocus on growth, but members pay to join and then give their time to the things they believe in and enjoy. And that's okay.

In 2019 I developed two new programmes to help existing business to grow and to create new jobs. One was getting groups of six entrepreneurs together and meeting bi-monthly for a day, to help each other solve their problems. This is much valued by members; an opportunity to share their problems and get support from their peers.

The second was to help entrepreneurs, who may be running out of energy and ideas, to find and unleash the entrepreneurs within their business. They help to develop the business and provide new ideas and energy.

I am immensely proud of what entrepreneurs in the region have created and achieved with what I regard as a good organisation.

Postscript

I resigned from the FEO board in October 2019 after ten years with the organisation. It is time for other entrepreneurs to move the organisation forward. I wish FEO all the best for the future.

Chapter Forty-Four

'Don't confuse me with the facts'

A **director of a new** client took me to one side and whispered, 'Fred (the CEO) thinks he is God's gift to management, but he lacks any self-insight. He is our biggest asset but also our biggest liability.' He then spoke with real frustration. 'He won't listen, makes rash impulsive decisions and changes his fucking mind daily.'

After our first a couple of meetings I agreed with him. I had decided the project was a non-starter. He was a nightmare.

Over forty years I have met several CEOs who have a total lack of self-awareness. I think it was Robert Burns who coined the phrase: '*O wad pow'r the gift gie us. To see oursels as others see us.*'

The personality strengths and weaknesses of the Leader are usually mirrored in the strengths and weaknesses of the business. Fact. That's why getting the right leader is a business-critical decision.

One feature of some CEOs and Leaders is their conviction that they are always right. That's okay if they are and are not betting the business on their ego. There is a difference between confidence, based on historical performance and egotistical arrogant swagger.

For example, when one of my clients Geoff Spencer of DB Schenker was confident in his role as CEO. His confidence was based on his deep understanding of the business, its people and culture. He had earned the right to be confident.

'I started at the bottom as a trainee train driver and have done just about every job in the business and excelled at them which may be why I am confident now.'

Contrast Geoff with Mr Michael, another client in this memoir who told me 'Hall, old chap my father handed me the reins when I was just twenty so it's in my blood you know.'

He was one of the 'born to rule brigade'.

He just about resisted patting me on the head.

Mr Michael reminded me of George Kelly's *Construct Theory*: 'We all see the world in our own individual idiosyncratic way which we believe is how it actually is. But everybody else, will also view the world in their own way, and they believe their view is the correct one.' Usually no amount of facts will change their world view.

Jim Collins, the author of the brilliant book *Good to Great*, says that the first signs of business failure are not a drop-in sales or profits but *complacency*. The belief that everything is okay, so there is no need to be concerned, change, or do anything different.

I see it often in businesses that were started twenty years ago or so, the owner has done quite well, they are comfortable, and their original drive and energy has all but disappeared. One entrepreneur said to me 'I have a nice house, kids at private school, I'm a member of the best golf club in the area, holiday home in Majorca, part of the local right social set and drive a top end car. What's not to like?'

So, it's understandable life is good, and they don't feel the need to change anything, even when people like me come along and try to persuade them about Jim Collins findings…

'Fuck off, I am doing very nicely thank you.'

Let's step back and try to figure out what's going on here.

Most entrepreneurs have ten to fifteen years in them, before they run out of energy passion and ideas; they maybe are coasting at best. They started the business, and many are very reluctant to let go of the reins.

When the world changes and threatens them or their business they regress to fight or flight. They basically reject it loudly or ignore it, putting their head in the sand.

Now you might think providing them with more facts might persuade them of their folly. Wrong. Their mantra appears to be: *Don't confuse me with the facts I have made my mind up.*

So, what's the answer?

Well my way, and this is not 'the only way', is to try and get them to trust me. I do this by delivering some short-term successes or helping them remove some headaches.

Sometimes, my track record helping some well-known businesses over forty years, helps establish my credibility.

Another strategy is to provide some feedback that shocks them out of their comfortable state. For example, an objectively completed Customer Perception Survey or Staff Survey often 'encourages' them to act.

But it's never easy, as my client of 35 years Terry Bramall said, 'You don't get to be CEO or owner of a business without a big ego. CEOs and owners cast a big shadow on the business and unless you find a way to help them to confront that; change is unlikely to happen.'

That's what I get paid for.

Chapter Forty-Five

Unleashing talent from within

A **client of mine, a** high-end gift retailer in North London, needed to improve cash flow and improve profits. His sales of a major product were falling, so we agreed to work on the problem together.

We interviewed some internal employees to lead the cost reduction project. A young management accountant, Jane, was the standout candidate. She was initially allocated a day a week to spend on the project, whilst maintaining her existing role.

She read my book, *Doing the Business*, which I wrote for Virgin Books with a forward by Richard Branson in 2002. It contains Toolkits which have been used by many other clients to revitalise their businesses, I have included some of them here. She identified those which would help her. See *Toolkit 9: Let Go to Grow* and *Toolkit 1: Working ON the Business*.

Over the years I had identified the benefits of looking outside your own industry sector for fresh ideas. My next step was to introduce Jane to another of my clients, a leader in the construction industry, so that she could 'pick their brains'. How, in their world, had they reduced their costs?

'I was impressed that they had learned to manage stock so tightly,' Jane reported. 'We have five years' stock, worth 700 thousand, which is never going to sell. So putting the stock into an attractive sale is an opportunity to cut our costs, reduce working capital and boost cashflow.'

I told Jane how I had helped my construction company client to set up efficiency groups, comprising of managers, buyers, engineers and accountants. These groups had successfully identified and made significant savings in purchasing, waste management, productivity on sites, and by minimising reworking.

Jane was impressed by this and decided to do the same. 'I loved the idea of setting up our own efficiency group to review the established practices that previously have never been challenged or changed. We've been so busy growing fast we forgot about cost-effectiveness – so there is plenty to go at!'

Jane selected four colleagues to work with her. Between them they uncovered several highly inefficient processes and practices. Amongst other things, they found ten years' worth of till rolls filling two cupboards!

'We discovered there seemed to have been no restrictions on ordering stock – anyone could do it with impunity.' Jane smiled ironically. 'Happy days for the suppliers! My team has now installed new processes that has brought order to our purchasing chaos.'

Next, I introduced Jane to another of my clients, a major supplier to the jewellery business who also owned several retail stores. They had recently taken cost-cutting measures, specifically by reworking staff rotas.

They confessed to Jane, 'Our stores were fully staffed on Mondays and Tuesdays, our quietest days, but we were short staffed at weekends, our busiest time, when we aimed to make seventy per cent of our weekly sales. Crazy.'

They addressed that issue and went further. They are now planning rotas by the hour rather than by the day, as had been their previous policy. Savings have been significant.

Jane's small group of managers and supervisors started to apply these new insights to their own operation and began to make significant savings.

She explains: 'I analysed all the costs on our P and L spreadsheets and questioned everything. For example, we had kept with several suppliers for many years, so I got three quotations for each product and was amazed at how much we could reduce our costs, simply by changing suppliers. We even switched auditors. I no longer believe there is such a thing as a fixed cost – everything can be improved upon.'

They benefitted further when the retail market took a dive in late 2018. By then the business was in much better shape to withstand any further drop in sales.

'Several of our big brand suppliers replicated some of our successful initiatives. This really helped with the process of developing partnerships with them. We got the credit for helping them.'

What lessons had Jane learned? What mistakes were made along the way?

'It wasn't all plain sailing,' she admitted. 'Firstly, a colleague went off sick, so I was dragged back to my normal accounting role. For a while, the improvement projects ground to a halt. Fortunately, our CEO recognised the financial benefits of the team's work, agreed to recruit an interim accountant and I returned to work on the projects.

'Secondly, it was very difficult to change people's behaviour.'

She went on. 'On reflection, to avoid hostility, we should have done a better job explaining that the project was about *cost saving* not *cost cutting*. There were unnecessary fears about job losses amongst our colleagues – a few raised hackles.

'Also, initially we didn't share information about the savings we had made very effectively, so we created a visual "thermometer" on the office wall which clearly illustrated our progress. Our colleagues liked that.

'We continued with the project and within eighteen months we saved the business over a million pounds, increasing our profits by twenty-five percent. The benefits will be carried forward into the coming years. The bonus is our work has significantly reduced our cost base forever.'

I asked Jane's boss if he was happy with the outcome.

He replied, 'Frankly, if Jane had not made the improvements she did so quickly, we might have gone out of business.'

Great work, Jane. Job done.

Doing the Business by David Hall – Virgin Books 2002

Chapter Forty-Six

Paul Sewell – The Sewell Group

Sometimes I come across a client who not only runs a good business but is also a good person. Dr Paul Sewell OBE, owner and Chairman of the Sewell Group, ticks both these boxes.

Paul's business is a multi-disciplined group of companies operating across Yorkshire. It includes thirteen filling stations and convenience stores, a construction business and an estates business (comprising investments, developments and facilities management).

In 2018 the business turned over £100 million and employed almost 500 hundred people.

Let's have a closer look at Paul's success. What qualities does he bring to the development of a good business?

Paul is an archetypal entrepreneur, spotting and grabbing opportunities and keeping red tape to a minimum; he is action-oriented, persistent and has a vision of the future for his business.

When I first visited him at his office in 2009, I was struck by the colourful posters that lined the walls, declaring inspirational statements like *Leaders don't create followers, they create more leaders; Customer Service is a way of life, not a Department.* And so on.

Paul said, 'Every year we visit other countries, typically the USA, Tokyo, Singapore, Hong Kong and Sydney Australia, to see what new ideas are emerging. In the States these posters are everywhere – they seem to play a part in supporting their business culture, so we brought back the idea.'

Two observations. For a long time I have preached that, if you want to develop your own business, go and see what *good* looks like. What are the top businesses doing? For some of the best models, go to the States (although China and India are catching up fast).

Secondly, other businesses have 'inspiring' slogans, largely ignored – not the case with employees of the Sewell Group. Paul lives by them, models them for others and insists that this is how he wants his business to behave. He provides *leadership* and I have seen the results for myself.

How does he get the best from his people?

'I believe we are following in the footsteps of GE and Zappos, in the States. Like they did, we get extraordinary performance from ordinary people, including myself. I believe that having the right culture is the key to business success. So we work hard to ensure we build and sustain the culture we want. It works for us.'

'How do you do it?'

'Firstly, we operate a "respect agenda", which means we treat everybody with dignity and appreciate them as individuals. We found that if you give respect first only then can you expect it back. This is a non-negotiable rule in our business; we get great performance as a result. It's not rocket science.

'We also train our people well. We give them very clear performance goals and promote from within, as a matter of principle. Many of our top team started here as apprentices or juniors and have grown with the business. We got into *The Times* "Top 100 Companies to work for" List every time we entered in 2009, 10 and 11, then 2018, when we were number one in Yorkshire (I think our people took real pride in that achievement!); and now 2020.'

'Impressive. Anything else?'

'We also have the annual Sewell Convention, a full week when we get all our people together to share our plans for the following year, put forward new ideas brought back from our visits to other great businesses, share our success and newfound wisdom – and generally to have fun!' He spreads his hands and smiles. See *Toolkit 3: Crafting Culture*.

'What's your role nowadays, Paul?'

'Having developed some good leaders in the company, I try to coach and support them. I visit our sites to ensure that we are living and breathing our values. Our workers are also co-shareholders, so I feel confident that they will look after their investments as well as mine.' See *Toolkit 9: Let Go to Grow*.

Clearly, Paul is a good businessman. So what about Paul as a person?

I am told that, to some people, he is a bit like Marmite – they either like him or not. I raise this with him.

'I've been told I'm a no nonsense straight talker, and some might find me a bit too assertive and, at times, dominating.'

I am in the 'like' camp – and here is why.

I have watched at close hand Paul's treatment of people. Very interpersonally skilled, he applies his 'respect agenda' unfailingly, dealing with his colleagues and contacts with dignity, without exceptions.

He is also a good leader: he sets the standards and values of the organisation and expects everyone else to live by them. He promotes from within, giving people, young and old, opportunities they may not find elsewhere. He trusts them to do their best and invariably they do.

There is no doubt that the Sewell Group is a unique business, led by an inspiring leader. Paul and his businesses deserve the success they now enjoy.

Chapter Forty-Seven

Getting the right people on the bus

I **am rereading Jim Collins** bestselling American business book *Good to Great*. His advice to 'Get the right people on the bus', chimes well with my recent survey of one hundred and fifty local business owners who suggested that finding good people, is the number one problem they face.

Typical comments from the survey:

'Finding good people is really holding the growth of my business back.'

'There is a shortage of young people with IT skills.'

'We can't get enough good engineers.'

'Young people don't have the right attitudes to work and just want to play on their mobiles.'

Tom Peters the management guru suggests that 'winning the war for talent' will be a priority for businesses in the next decade.

I thought I had better investigate, as finding good people appears to be a problem many of my client's face.

'Sherlock Holmes investigates....'

Individual responses to the survey, revealed that they have different recruitment issues. Different businesses needed different skills and experiences; engineering was a hot spot in the region. Ironically, a number had recruited highly skilled engineers from Europe/overseas, particularly from Poland, who were returning home because of potential Brexit implications.

In desperation several businesses led by Charlie Spencer, owner of the Spencer Engineering Group, have just established their own college in Hull. The Ron Dearing university technical college 'aims to help people gain the qualifications, skills and experience that employers are looking for.'

Neil Fisher, owner of Airco, a refrigeration and air conditioning business were, so dissatisfied with the quality of the training of engineers who he hired that he set up his own training school to retrain engineers to his required standards.

Thinking about the attitudes of young people, it seems to me, that some employers want 'oven ready' people lining up to fill jobs. Well if it is a problem, you can't change parenting, but what you can do is to actively try to attract young people with the right attitudes to work.

Matt Das of Eon Media, a modern marketing business has made the effort to go into schools and colleges and deliver exciting presentations about his business. Pupils call him seeking vacation opportunities and now he has a pipeline of young people who have spent time in his business, so he has found out about them and vice versa. Matt has created a way to solve his recruitment problem, hiring six new people per year.

The third group of people that the survey reveals has a problem is the lack of good sales people. This is a problem many businesses have, as one client put it 'we have several sales people but only one who can really sell.'

This fits with my experience of clients who are desperate to make sales but limited by having low quality sales people. It's also clear that when people do find a good salesperson, they make sure they keep them by treating them well, they don't want to leave and so it's difficult to entice them to join your business. Conversely the mediocre are like Bedouins moving from job to job. There is no easy answer to this dilemma.

One thing however that can be done to help is to provide the front line sales resources with effective support: telesales, good customer research, technical back up, product literature, etc. In other words, make it as easy as possible for sales people to sell.

One possibility is to attend trade shows and seek out the good sales people there and try to headhunt them.

There are no easy answers to this problem, but I have discovered you need to work at it and if you do this well, it is often the key to unlock your chance of success.

Chapter Forty-Eight

Football Crazy

The **League One football** club, Doncaster Rovers, was owned by a long-term client and friends of mine, Terry Bramall and the late Dick Watson. Their business was based in Doncaster, so they thought it would be a nice idea to support the town, by investing in the club, and getting some positive PR for the business.

Dick and I worked on the five year strategy for the club and we also facilitated several business improvement projects, including boosting ticket sales, sorting out the board of directors and improving the profitability of the club.

Not every project we worked on together was a success.

I facilitated the recruitment process for a new football manager.

We advertised the position in the Football League Managers journal and were immediately inundated with applications for the job including a recent England Manager, who wanted a £1.5m salary. The post was being offered at 150k, so a bit out of our league. He was not that good anyway, even with England.

We had a manager of an existing club in Scotland who announced to the media that he was favourite for the job. He had not applied for it. Apparently, it's a regular scam. They then approach their Chairman and demand a pay rise to stay!

Having cut the candidates down to the two, we begin the interviewing process.

The first candidate arrived wearing a big hat and massive sunglasses. He crept into the room looking around and whispered, 'I don't think anybody spotted me.' He then told us how much he was looking forward to moving back south, from Scotland, and joining either Barnsley or Sheffield United.

Next...

The second candidate was impressive. He told us he had watched the Rovers several times and had already prepared training schedules for individual players to match their strengths and weaknesses. He said that he had breakfast last week with Sir Alex (Ferguson) of Manchester United, who had promised him some loan players.

He revealed that whilst playing for a premier league club, his job was to pick fights with the opponents if things weren't going well. This is the clue to his attitude that we missed...

We appointed him. All the selection panel were impressed with him.

Six months later he was fired as he turned out to be bloody useless. He alienated all the players, seemed clueless on tactics and clearly had a drink problem.

Not one of my better days as a consultant.

Lessons learned from this experience: check candidates out more thoroughly, particularly those who name drop top people like Sir Alex Ferguson.

If candidates sound too good to be true, they probably are.

Get the players involved in the selection process. They will probably suss out the bullshitters.

Don't be impressed by football players who played at the top level. If somebody has little previous management experience you are taking a big risk.

I know we should have done these things, but this guy romanced us, and we fell for it.

Later, David Blunt, Dick's co-director, took over the Chairmanship of the club. He has done an excellent job delivering success for Doncaster. Together we jointly delivered several improvement projects. An interesting one was investigating why in the 2016 season the club were winning most matches away from home but losing many home games. This is not the normal pattern of results, it's usually the other way around.

We assembled a small group of people, the Manager, Chairman and CEO and we thought it would help to include the club captain James Coppinger. I asked several questions trying to figure out the answer to this puzzle. Not a great deal of response from the group. We were about to give up so in desperation I confronted James,

'Okay if I put a gun to your head and said what's up with playing at home and by the way ignore the fact the Chairman and Manager are sat here (footballers are normally very deferential to the management) what would you say?'

He looked around nervously and then quietly said, 'The view of the boys in the dressing room is when we run out at home it is deadly quiet, we don't have a rousing anthem like other clubs. We can't hear the crowd cheering it's like playing in empty stadium, they are too spread out in small groups.'

'Good, anything else James?'

'Well, ere yes, the dressing rooms are bare concrete walls no pictures or excitement.'

He was on a roll now.

'And our dressing rooms are the largest and best equipped in the league, our opponents love coming here to play. That's it.'

Wow. Got it.

The club set up a competition with the fans to find a rousing song. They closed parts of the ground so fans gathered in large groups and their singing and chanting could be heard.

Large pictures of the players and their glory days were put up in the dressing rooms and corridors.

I suggested making the away dressing rooms less comfortable like painting it dark brown and turning the hot water off in the showers, but I think this was put on hold...

Did it work?

The results did improve at home but hard to say it was down to what we did. Maybe the fact that the players felt their voices had been listened to might have helped?

Lesson: if you really want to know what's happening ask the people involved, at the sharp end.

Chapter Forty-Nine

Service on the phone

'**D**ial 1 to place an order; 2 to check a delivery; 3 to add new items and 4 just in case you intend to shoot yourself, due to our piss-poor service!'

Don't you just hate automatic 'customer service' systems? You hang on as the minutes tick by and get so angry you can't speak to a human being to vent your frustrations.

However, I bring hope.

Having suffered at the hands of the Sad West Bank for years (strange isn't it how we put up with crap service from banks for most of our lives) my wife, sick of my tantrums, suggested I gave her bank a try.

So, I duly call First Direct (those who bank with First Direct can stop reading here as you know what's coming next). Businesses who currently provide lousy customer care on the telephone, listen up.

I call First Direct and get to speak to a real human being.

'Mr Hall. Welcome to First Direct.'

Wow! It was a fantastic experience from that moment. Helpful. Courteous. Polite. Professional. Not pushy. They must have done their research: What do customers hate about the service they get from their bank? Right okay, we will do the opposite. I thought I had been transported to another planet. Brilliant service from the first contact.

They are so good that I call them up when Ellen and I have a row. It's much better than the Relate Counselling Service.

'Hello, Mr Hall, fallen out with Ellen again? Never mind we have some good news for you. We're increasing your interest rate, so you get more for your money.'

(I made this bit up, but honestly, they are this good).

I guess you notice more when you get a stark contrast between poor and excellent service.

I was so impressed I wanted to find out how they did it, so I visited them at their HQ in Leeds. I meet Joe, dressed in smart jeans a white button-down shirt and wearing a broad smile.

'Welcome to First Direct Mr Hall. You've been a customer of ours since last March, how are you finding our service?'

'Bloody brilliant Joe – and that's why I am here.'

I recount my previous experiences of banks. To be fair to Sad West, most banks are as bad as each other. But it's not just banks that deliver poor service. Can you think of the last time you were delighted with any service you received? I digress. Back to Joe.

'So how do you consistently provide such outstanding personal customer service?'

Joe's smile widens, 'Well we don't have any physical high street branches so our only contact with our customers is via the telephone or internet. So, our telephone service has to be top notch.'

'But how do you do it?'

'Well we have a secret, but I will share it. We hire nice people and nice people are generally nice to customers. We originally tried hiring bankers and then tried to train them to be nice to our customers. That didn't work. We now hire nice people and then train them in our systems and processes.' See *Toolkit 6: Getting Your Customer Service Right* and *Toolkit 5: Delighting Customers.*

'It takes six weeks of intensive training, with coaches listening in on their calls and providing feedback and guidance, before we let them loose on our customers.'

So, that's how they do it. Hard work and a lot of effort but, my God it works superbly.

First Direct consistently win most of the awards for customer service in banking. Well deserved.

I guess the messages are to other service providers is invest in delighting your customers and you will be rewarded with repeat business and new customers through recommendations. And, to long-suffering bank customers don't put up with it. Change your bank.

As I drive home from Leeds, I notice I have a wide smile on my face, that's the First Direct effect.

Chapter Fifty

Doing the 'Right Thing' pays dividends

I have one client who provides me with my own office, pays for a car park slot and provides my favourite coffee, when I visit them. Oh and always pays my bills on time. Consequently I am constantly thinking of ways to help her to improve her business.

This got me thinking about people who do the 'Right Thing', why do they do it and does it pay off?

A key principle, I believe is that businesses *should* do the right thing and seek to balance the interests of Colleagues, Customers, and Investors. If one of these groups gets too powerful or too weak the business can fail.

For example, the trade unions were too powerful in the seventies, demanding excessive wage rises; several businesses failed, including the coal industry.

Greedy investors or top managers can create major crisis i.e. Persimmons CEO who recently had to resign because of the extraordinary share option payments he received.

Finally customers can be cheated by monopoly businesses; for example landlords continually putting up prices today in 2020 when there is no real justification other than them trousering more profit.

So one concept of doing the right thing at a strategic level maybe to seek to maintain a fair balance between colleague, customer and investor interests.

This was a key factor in the success of Sir Richard Branson's Virgin business. His view is: 'let's look after our colleagues, who will then look after our customers who will look after us, the investors.'

Does treating colleagues with dignity and respect, pay off in terms of engagement, commitment and performance?

My experience suggests it does in spades.

Most people don't come to work to do a bad job. The majority want to be proud of the organisation they work for, as it says something about them, 'I am okay, I work for a good business, I am not wasting my life.'

If a business treats people with dignity and respect, they often produce results beyond expectations.

As a manager in IBM told me 'the magic of our business is, we seem to get extraordinary performance from ordinary people.'

It's about designing the Culture you want so you don't get one you don't want. See *Toolkit 3: Crafting Culture.*

How about customers?

Twenty years ago providing a level of efficient, polite customer service was good enough for most customers as they had no other benchmark experiences. Then businesses like First Direct, the bank, recognised that if they delivered outstanding customer service that delighted their customers, they had a powerful competitive advantage.

Latterly businesses like Amazon have redefined how easy and quickly customers can order and receive goods the next day. This has reset the bar for customer expectations for everybody else.

In the late 90's smart businesses like Keepmoat, realised that if they went a step further and built strong partnerships with their customers by helping them to achieve their goals. This win-win approach paid off for customers and suppliers. Partnering means helping customers deliver their goals. This is the ultimate in competitive advantage.

How about Investors? A personal view: Investors who are in it for the long run generally get more commitment and performance from their employees if they believe the business is in it for the long run. The biggest stress for most people is not knowing if they have a future. Family businesses normally provide some comfort to deal with this uncertainty.

In my career I always try to encourage clients to do the right thing.

My experience is that businesses that try to the right thing for their employees, customers and investors generally get the rewards they deserve.

Maybe in 2020 doing the right thing could become competitive advantage in an increasingly fast moving and changing world, by providing comfort and certainty to customers, employees, and investors.

Chapter Fifty-One

A hair-raising experience

I'm sitting in front of a new client in his posh London office. His business manufactures garments for major fashion retailers, including Marks and Spencer.

He is in his late fifties, smartly dressed, wearing a pale blue shirt with a white collar. There is something a bit weird about people who wear shirts with different coloured collars, don't you think? He has luxuriant bright red hair, parted meticulously to the side.

I try to ask him some opening questions: he is very defensive.

'So, what do you think you can tell me about my business, son? I've been at it thirty years.'

I try to be nice. 'I was told you had a few issues. I'd be grateful for some more background.'

He folds his arms, leans back in his chair. 'All right. As you probably know, we are – or were – a major supplier to Marks and Spencer, who promote their brand with a policy of selling only British-made goods. We were required to sew into every shirt and garment a "Made in the UK" label. This was fine until we found a cheaper way of making our products in Sri Lanka. Unfortunately, our big mistake was to continue labelling the garments "Made in the UK".' He glances away.

'Oh dear.' I try to sound sympathetic. Can they really have been that stupid?

'As a result,' he pauses, swallowing, 'M&S "deselected" us and we lost a major part of our business.'

As he speaks, I notice he constantly twiddles a pencil in his hands. As he gets more agitated, he twiddles faster. Eventually he snaps the pencil in half and bends down to pick up the pieces. His thatch of ginger hair also falls onto the floor. Without missing a beat, he picks it up, places it back on his head and carries on talking as if nothing has happened.

I nearly choke and pretended to cough. This can't get any worse, can it? Yes, it can.

His office door is flung open and an irate young woman bursts in, screaming at him.

'You bastard! You were seen out with your wife again! You promised me....'

He stands up hastily, knocking back his chair. 'Yes darling, but I told you ...'

She interrupts, wagging a shaking finger. 'No, no, no! I warned you – if you want me, then she is history.' At this point, I get up very quietly and tiptoe out of the room. They don't even notice.

I thank his secretary on my way out and head for the underground station, pondering on the events of the last hour. Some jobs are not worth doing and this is one of them.

Postscript

A month later, I learned that this gentleman had disappeared to southern Spain, allegedly to avoid paying huge debts to his suppliers and HMRC.

Chapter Fifty-Two

Developing Designs

I met Rob Daysley at a business conference I am speaking at in 2019.

'I could do with you having a look at my business and help me to develop it,' he said.

I didn't know him personally so I suggested as I was leaving, 'email me and I will get back to you.'

The next morning before nine he called me directly. He seemed a good guy, so I invited him to meet me at 'Cowshed HQ', my home office at Hotham.

He arrives early for our meeting; so he was either keen or desperate. He is a tall guy six foot four I guess, lean and looks fit.

'Okay Rob, tell me about you and your business.'

'I left school in 1993 and wrote to several sign writing businesses seeking a job. One offered me an interview and then an apprenticeship immediately.'

'What did you do to impress him?'

'Well I hand-wrote my applications calligraphically, he really liked that. I worked for the business for two years learning the trade. But I was always pushed by family to learn the business and go on my own. The opportunity arose when one of the customers saw the potential in me and offered me the opportunity to work with them to get started. I worked out of my Dad's garage to begin with.'

'Hold on a minute Rob; how did your employer react to you stealing one of his clients?'

'Well obviously he wasn't happy. He didn't speak to me again for years.'

'And how do you feel about what you did now, Rob?'

'Looking back, maybe I didn't handle it so well at the time, but I was just seventeen at the time and I guess I was naïve and a bit manic, so maybe that got in the way of me acting in a proper manner?

'I did really well, having fun and making plenty of money. So at twenty I decide to have a year off and have even more fun, doing what I liked. Then I realised the money was running out, so I had better get back to work. I bought a vinyl cutter with my last 10k and found a small business unit. I had no customers.'

'How did you find customers, Rob?'

'I knew a few people, so I started getting work doing vans and then black cabs. I got a good name, customers liked me.

'Then out of the blue a guy called me, his FD had stopped at the newsagents opposite my unit for cigarettes, he had seen my sign and written down the number. He gave it to the buyer who he knew was struggling with their supply chain.

'The buyer asked me, "Do you do signage for ambulances?"

'"Yes of course" I said. I didn't know anything about ambulances. I got an order for 5 ambulances then another 27, I had to buy a 60k bespoke machine to do it with money I didn't have... and now we are in the top 5 ambulance signage providers in the country.

'Our sports business came from a visit to the KCOM football stadium in Hull in 2003. I had been working with the club and they agreed I could do the work on the new stadium. To get the business I had to partner with the club and sponsor them for 10k, again I didn't have the money. The work was good, but I needed to get a unit three times the size of the one I had and employ five more people.'

'You were off and flying, Rob.'

'Not quite yet; then another break. The stadium was for both rugby and football. The rugby team placed rotating advertising boards around the ground and surprise surprise the football team wanted the same. I tried to create my own with difficulty, spent a load of money and ended up agreeing a deal with the rugby provider solving the problem and becoming the leading rotating signage company in the UK,' he says with pride.

'I bought a building in 2007 to accommodate our growth.

'By 2008 I had achieved my goals: more than £1m sales and I own my own building. But then I got complacent we let it slip and faced big pay rises and the recession.

'In 2013 I bought another signage company and integrated it into our core business.'

Rob has the typical entrepreneur characteristics as set out in my last book; Entrecode (2013)*. That book is the result of ten years research into how entrepreneurs really do create successful businesses.

The way Rob operates is typically entrepreneurial: Find a customer problem solve it, then sell the solution to others. But Rob goes further. He usually has no idea how to solve the problem nor the resources to do it. But somehow, he always finds a way.

Robs other characteristic is that he prefers to get out of trouble rather than stay out of trouble. I have noticed this trait in many entrepreneurs.

He admits to getting bored when things are going smoothly, he needs the buzz of crisis to motivate him. At times he seems to almost create a crisis, to get him out of bed on a morning.

Rob is also an options thinker, so typical of successful entrepreneurs; if plan A doesn't work, he can quickly create plan B then C etc. He never gets stuck.

Add to this his personal drive, enthusiasm and ability to romance people to get what he wants. Rob is a Rock Star archetypal entrepreneur.

Fast forward to 2019. This is where I help Rob.

I agree to help him for four months to work on his business.

He told me, 'I think I need some more entrepreneurial energy in my business we have got a bit stale.'

'Okay Rob do you have any entrepreneurs within your business right now that we could mobilise?'

'I have two guys who are very good, I think they could be internal entrepreneurs.'

'Shall we find out if they are Rob?'

We agree to put them to work on some opportunities to improve his business. I provide them with the *Toolkit 7: Intrapreneurship*, to help them.

They conducted a customer survey in just one week (normally it takes a month) and identified the businesses strengths and weaknesses which they quickly started to address.

He simplified and standardised the pricing process and trained estimators to use it.

Tenders were analysed to see why they lost opportunities and the results created a different approach to winning work.

At this point the team was joined by the sales director who began the process of business development right across the UK.

He began by partnering with key customers which creates significant new opportunities.

His leadership of the sales team is brilliant: encouraging, supporting and driving them.

This team produces results way beyond expectations in record time, compared to other clients. They were hard working, smart and delivered. They are proper intrapreneurs.

Robs view: 'This project far exceeded all our expectations; the business is in a much stronger place than it was. The guys have been magnificent. They have brought new opportunities and renewed my own mojo. I am really confident in our future.'

Final thought. I hope Rob does not revert to type and deliberately throw a spanner in the works to create the crisis he thrives on!

*Entrecode: Unlocking the entrepreneurial DNA. Management Books 2000 Ltd

Chapter Fifty-Three
Hugh Rice the Jewellers

Have you noticed sometimes that the harder you try and the more desperate you get; you just can't seem to get anywhere? Frustrating. Then other times, when you are half asleep, things fall into your lap.

At a meeting of For Entrepreneurs Only, I was approached by a man who introduced himself as Mike Rice the Chairman and majority shareholder of Hugh Rice Jewellers. I have no idea who he is. He is a large, rotund individual with greying hair, a trendy short beard and a cheeky grin. I quickly decided that I liked him (an important issue for me these days). After talking for a while, we agreed that I will help him create a long-term plan.

'Will you come and help us devise a strategy for our business?' he said.

My first response: 'Have you got any money?'

It is spontaneous, and I wish I had not said it quite the way I did.

He looks me straight in the eye and smiles.

'We are a very profitable business; we want to build on that success and grow it.'

Mike told me a bit about the history of his business and his ambition to grow it. The Hugh Rice (HR) board consists of four working Rice family members and a non-family finance director. Paul the Managing Director is Hugh's (the founder) son, Danielle, the operations director his daughter and James, Mike's son, is the Marketing Director.

Alarm bells started to ring. My experiences of family businesses are mixed at best. They usually start off like the Waltons (happy days) but many end up like the Borgias (carnage). I have one family business client who signs off his emails: Borgia Bill!

I wonder how the HR project will unfold: Waltons or the Borgias?

The solution to not disintegrating into a Borgia family nightmare is to set up a legally binding family charter BEFORE things go pear-shaped. Many families don't believe this will be needed – before the crisis – 'we all get on like a house on fire.' But when the house is on fire, it's usually too late. However, on the upside, family businesses, unlike many private equity owned businesses, are normally in it for the long run and this gives confidence to both employees and suppliers.

There is something I always find quite exciting about the first day you start to work with a new client. You never know what's going to happen: Are they up for it? Are they serious or just going through the motions? You'd imagine that having hired me to do a job that they would be serious, but you never can tell....

Mike had been a bit vague about the details of the business's history, so I thought I would fill in the gaps by asking Paul, the Managing Director.

'Give me a quick summary of the history of the business please, Paul?'

'The business was started in 1971 by Mike's brother Hugh, with a two-hundred-pound bank loan, in a small basement in George Street in Hull. Hugh served his apprenticeship as a horologist repairing clocks and watches.

'Mike joined the business in 1974, having served a Jewellery apprenticeship. In 1988 the business moved to a larger premise in George street where it was doing 50% retail sales and 50% servicing clocks and watches. The turnover at the time was £1.7 million, they were making a good living. I joined the business in 1997.'

'When did the move to St Stephens happen, it must have been a big step to take?'

He smiled, as if recalling the day, it happened.

'It was a massive risk, we moved in 2007 to bigger premises in the new mall in the centre of Hull. This enabled us to attract wealthier customers and sell more up-market brands.'

'Tell me a bit about acquiring the Pandora franchise?'

He got up from his chair and stared out of the window.

'Our big break came in 2009 when we took on the 4th Pandora franchise in the UK. Pandora now have 200 stores, so we were in at the start. Since 2009 we have opened nine Pandora outlets, they have been fabulously successful for us.'

This was a business that takes big risks, then works out how to make it work, typically entrepreneurial.

I worked with the board and they enthusiastically completed a five-year strategy. They decided to print a copy of it on cards and give them to all their colleagues. They also displayed it on three huge 3 x 4 metre boards, in every store. See *Toolkit 10: Redoing Your Strategy to Revitalise Your Business.*

A briefing was planned to explain it to all colleagues. Think this is the norm in business? Think again. This level of communications between the directors and everybody else is very unusual in my experience. So, a good job, well done.

Now here's the thing. This experience suggested to me that the HR family were smart, hard working and fully engaged in the business, no Borgia clues.

But to succeed a business also needs to design its culture, or way of doing things – you either get a culture by design, one you want, or by default, one you don't want.

Once again, the HR team did an excellent job of determining the way they wanted their business to behave. These guys proved very easy to work with; it's a joy to help people low on ego high on humility, and I am getting paid for it. See *Toolkit 3: Crafting Culture.*

Fast forward: I heard nothing from them for a few months. Then, one morning the phone rang it was Paul Rice, and after a few pleasantries he got straight to the point.

'David, we are ambitious, as you know, and want to move our business from good to great. We need help to do that, starting with delivering the strategy we designed twelve months ago.'

'What have you done about delivering it?' I asked.

'Honestly? Well, not a lot, but we are keen, and we recognise we need help.'

I was impressed with Paul's honesty and his humility, refreshingly different from CEOs with big egos, who feel unable to ask for help, as it might suggest a sign of weakness. So, I bet he won't make the mistake of expecting things to happen, as if by magic.

My most effective clients understand their own strengths and weaknesses, are open to learning and generally take the actions agreed. A rare breed.

Over a very boozy dinner, Mike, Paul and I shook hands on a deal. I will help them until 2020 on a retained basis, with an incentive performance bonus. Happy days.

Some businesses seem to think that having designed a strategy, that's it job done. But that's the easy bit. Taking the tough decisions is what's required to build a successful business; getting the wrong people off the bus; exiting 'favourite' loss making products or markets; raising finance to grow the business, these are generally the things that keeps people awake at night.

We all hoped to replicate the successes achieved with my favourite client, Keepmoat. I never thought I would ever get back to those the most exciting of my career.

Somebody up there must like me....

I have discovered over time that most businesses only need to focus on three things in the first year, to start to deliver their strategy. It was clear that improving the profit margin, developing their people and controlling fixed costs were the things HR needed to work on. A project champion was selected for each (somebody with their neck on the line).

To get some traction into the projects, Whiteboards were displayed in the board room, with the planned actions, to help monitor and manage progress.

This business did not have a track record of working ON the business in this way, they were normally busy working IN it. But no business can improve if it just continues to do what it has always done. This was major culture change, if the business was to achieve its goals.

Several projects were undertaken in each of the three project areas: discounting was reviewed to improve margin; a HR Academy was established to develop the people and a capital investment process was installed to control fixed costs. Significant improvements in the business were made quickly as a result. The team's confidence in the future was increasing by the day.

The future looked bright!

Listening to Radio Four – another gloomy news story: the UK retail sector had taken another dive. Major retailers were going into administration and the High Street appeared to be in terminal decline. Hugh Rice was not immune, sales and cash flow are both affected. The hope was that it was a short-term blip, but we were all disappointed: sales continued a downward track, alarm bells rang, something had to be done and quickly.

The first lifebelt thrown, was to create a 'Runner': the aim, to cut costs and to get control of the cash position. See *Toolkit 4: Cut Costs & Increase Profits.*

This might be worthy of a bit of elaboration.

Samantha Paddison, a working mum with her own personal challenges, was selected as the Runner. She was clearly used to juggling priorities and multitasking both at home and at work as a chartered accountant leading the finance team. Sam was selected because she had the skills required by a Runner: methodical, analytical, hardworking, respected in the business and most importantly keen to do the job.

She was asked to be the Runner for two days a week, as well as covering her other responsibilities – the old maxim if you want anything doing give it to a busy person.

It quickly became clear that major cost saving opportunities could only be delivered if Sam took on the Runner role full time. So, a new management accountant was hired to backfill Sam's original role.

Sam immediately uncovered some major opportunities to reduce costs and conserve cash. The big early wins were matching staff numbers and stock costs directly to sales. This resulted in a saving of over one million pounds; to put this into context it was 50% of the forecasted profits for the year.

The next phase was based on an insight from another client, who was making sixteen per cent profits. When asked how he did it, he replied, 'easy, sixty-four quarters of a percent.' In other words look after the pennies and the pounds will look after themselves.

In twelve months, thirty projects were identified and successfully delivered, for example re-negotiating supplier contracts, cutting cleaning costs, changing IT providers, reducing spend on stationary. Several projects provided real competitive advantage, so cannot be reported, without giving away too much. See *Toolkit 1: Working ON the Business*

At the same time, it was decided to improve sales to protect cash flow. An experienced jewellery sales trainer was hired, and all sales staff went through an intensive sales training programme lasting twelve months. This resulted in improvements to sales and cash flow.

2018 had been a tough year for Hugh Rice but they responded magnificently.

As a result of the downturn in retail sales, Paul Rice decided to revisit the strategy we created in 2015. Lots had happened in the past three years that had made the original plan less relevant. We developed a new strategy which is much more aligned with the current economic retail climate.

The board members then produced a business plan for each of their departments, to cascade the strategy into the business.

I asked Paul Rice how he would summarise the HR journey from Good to Great thus far?

He grimaced, 'We have been on a roller coaster of a journey over the past eighteen months with all the work we have put in to develop the business, 40 plus improvement projects and counting.

'We are like many others in the Retail sector, we got caught in the big downturn in sales in 2017 it was unexpected and threw our forecasts up in the air.

'There is no doubt we could have been in big trouble if Sam, our brilliant Runner, had not uncovered a treasure trove of cash and reduced our costs significantly.

'Then three major problems hit the business at once. Pandora sales were significantly lower than expected, the stock position was a lot worse than had been forecast and costs were increasing, rents, rates, wages.

'Sales down costs up is the worst of all worlds.

'In order to keep the bank onside, further significant cost savings needed to be made.'

It has been a torrid, stressful time for the Rice family.

They made more positive changes to their business in a very short period, than any client I have ever worked with. At a time when the Retail sector has been in meltdown the family has really pulled together. Very brave and frankly heroic in my opinion.

Waltons or Borgias? Neither, just a hard-working family business who work hard, play hard and enjoy working together.

They deserve to succeed.

A 'Runner' is a term I invented to distinguish it them from other traditional business roles. It is somebody given the responsibility and authority to inspect and reduce every cost in the business. The principle is 'no fear or favour', so nothing is off limits. Dangerous territory for any manager of a nervous disposition; what will they find on my patch?

Chapter Fifty-Four

Profitable Partnering

One of the ways I try to help clients make a step change in their business performance, is to introduce them to 'what great looks like'. One process in particular, Profitable Partnering has proved highly effective typically with customers and suppliers.

I helped Hugh Rice Jewellers, to cut costs and gain competitive advantage by partnering with key suppliers. Partnering involves getting close to suppliers or customers, treating them with respect and helping them to build their own businesses. You then enjoy the benefits of becoming a preferred supplier or customer.

Many businesses treat suppliers and even customers like the enemy. When they take a partnering approach they stand out and people want to do businesses with them.

I introduced James Rice, the marketing director of Hugh Rice, to an old client and good friend, Dave Hughes. Dave was a quantity surveyor who migrated into commercial management. Together we developed a process of partnering, which helped Keepmoat secure some long-term profitable relationships with both their customers and suppliers.

James wanted to develop stronger bonds with his key suppliers to gain competitive advantage. I felt James would benefit from Dave's experiences.

I had not seen Dave for four years, so we began with a bit of banter, as friends often do.

'Morning, Dave. Wow, you've lost more hair than when I saw you last!'

'Aye, and you never had any,' he says, running his hand through his thinning hair and laughing.

After the pleasantries, we recap on the Partnering process, which we worked on together.

See *Toolkit 1: Working ON the Business.*

Dave started, 'Firstly, we decided which suppliers we wanted to work with long term. We then identify who the key people were in each supplier. The next step is to categorise each individual Red, Amber or Green.'

I joined in: 'Red means we don't know them, no contact, never done business with them. Amber is we've met them, done some business, but we are not really very close to them. Green, we know them well, done a lot of business and we could do more, and we meet often. They call us regularly, we are friends.'

I noticed James is taking copious notes as we talk.

'What do you think is the final step in partnering, James?' Dave asks.

'Erm, well I guess you need more Greens,' James replies.

'Spot on. The challenge for the business is to turn all the contacts green' says Dave in a determined manner.'

'Bloody hell that's sounds a lot of work', James gasps.

'It is, but tell James the benefits Keepmoat enjoyed Dave, when you turned your key contacts green and started Partnering.'

'Well, we maintained deliveries of products when supplies were tight, which enabled us to keep building, whilst our competitors went short of supplies. We also got preferential rebate terms and better trading terms. At the same time, we were negotiating better prices based on guaranteed volumes over a twelve-month period.'

I couldn't resist: 'Partnering equal Profits, James,' I said with a smile.

'Where the hell did that come from,' responds Dave, with a large grin on his face.

'How many people were involved in the process?' asks James.

'We tried to link up our people and the suppliers at the same levels. So, buyer to buyer, operations directors to their senior people, admin staff with their admin people.'

I quickly add, 'Clearly not everybody is comfortable building relationships so you have to find out pretty quickly who can and who can't deliver the partnering way of doing business.'

James leans forward in his chair, 'I can see us really benefitting if we can make it work with our major brands'.

'Yes, we did it with our supply chain and it worked brilliantly,' says Dave proudly.

As we stand up to leave James has a big smile on his face, as if he had just won the lottery.

'Wow thanks guys, that was really helpful.'

I said, 'Thanks Dave I owe you one, I'll treat you to a nice meal.'

He rolls his eyes, 'Yeah a Big Mac like last time. No thanks!'

Chapter Fifty-Five

A friend in need is a ....

When I first started my consulting practice nearly forty years ago, a wise friend, Gerry Egan, gave me a piece of advice: 'Never take on a project for a family member, or a friend. You may live to regret it.'

For thirty years I heeded his advice…. until now.

I got a call from a lifelong friend, let's call him Jon.

'David, I have left my job as a surveyor and bought a pub. It has a restaurant. It's got loads of potential. I know you have worked with several restaurants; will you come and help me get it up and running?'

Oh dear, I really like Jon, but I feel conflicted. In one ear I hear Gerry …. 'You may live to regret it…'

Not sure why Jon wants my help? He knows I work with entrepreneurs; does he just want to impress me that he too is an entrepreneur?

Jon has helped me in the past, so after some deliberation, I decide to break Gerry's rule.

I arrive at Jon's pub hoping this will be a quick fix. It is a two hour drive up to a remote part of North Yorkshire. 'Great, isn't it?' says Jon as he greets me with a huge smile on his face. 'Got a great deal on it,' he proudly tells me.

Having been shown around the place I can see why the previous owner might have been glad to do 'a deal'. It looks tired, in need of serious refurbishment. The carpets are soiled and threadbare. The Victorian looking red flock wallpaper creates the dark, dank feel of a funeral parlour, rather than a thriving pub. It smells faintly of urine.

I ask myself; would I like to eat and drink here? The answer is a definite NO.

I decide I owe it to Jon, as a friend, to be straight with him, just as I would with any paying client.

'I expect nothing else from you,' he said, 'that's why I asked you to have a look at us.'

'Have you ever had any experience in running a pub or restaurant, Jon?'

'No, but I have always fancied it, being my own boss.'

'Where do you intend to start, to make this a success?'

'New carpets and re decorate it throughout. I can't afford any major building work; I just need to get it looking clean and loved a bit. I want to refit the bar. I got an architect mate to come up with a plan, but it looks expensive. What do you think?'

'Good start, it is not a very appealing place right now. What about the people you have inherited; chefs, waiting and bar staff?'

'A few have left and having met them I am quite pleased they did. I have found a young lad, who has done some cooking, so I intend to give him a go in the kitchen. We will try to get some local students to serve in the restaurant.'

'Whoa Jon, you are about to make the classic mistake that most would be restauranteurs make.

You need to invest in good staff right now and not in a new bar. You need a chef who can cook food properly and friendly, efficient staff who can look after your customers. That way customers will come back regularly; they will also tell their friends and your place will be heaving.'

'Yes but....'

'No "yes buts", Jon. You asked for my advice that's it. It's your business, not mine, so you can do what you like.'

I wondered if I had been too honest with him...

He looks a little sheepish, is he ready for my next question?

'How do you intend to market "The Jolly Rodger"? It's bloody miles from anywhere.'

'Ah, I've got a young college student to knock me up a bit of a website.'

'For fuck's sake, Jon, you desperately need customers. Do you honestly think a website designed by a young student is going to drag them in from miles around?'

Oh dear, he looks even more sheepish...

No holding back now, 'Okay you asked me here to advise you Jon, so here is what I would suggest you do.

'First, get the decorating done asap. Hire a decent chef with the money you will save from the bar refit. Find some waiting staff who have good people skills and train them in the way you want them to serve your customers. Set the standards you expect from day one.

'Then I suggest you get some local students to drop leaflets at local villages, inviting people to a free barbecue and drinks on a weekend to celebrate the opening of the "New Jolly Roger". This normally brings people in, even if just to have a nosey and get a free beer.

'Once you are up and running and have cash rolling in, you can think about investing in a decent website.

'I have suggested to other restaurants they invite restaurant journalists from the local newspapers to visit them. We just need to think of some good reasons to get them here.

'I noticed on my way here a large industrial estate. So invite the PAs of the bosses to a free lunch; they are the ones who normally book events for their businesses. This has also worked well for others.

'If I were you, I would also go and visit some successful pubs and restaurants and learn from them. What are they doing? How do they get people to visit them?

'I have noticed that restaurateurs do talk to each other and share ideas, it's unusual in other businesses but they do help each other so join up with the local owners.

'Now, as I said before, it's your business you do what you want, but these ideas have worked well. These are just my thoughts. What do you think?'

He looks past me, not catching my eye and sighs, 'Sounds like a lot of work, David.'

'Yes, it is, there are no quick fixes or magic answers as far as I know. I wish there were my friend.'

'Well, I will think about it. But I still think I will do the website and invest in the bar refit. I can cover the cooking in the short term. But thanks for coming David appreciate it. Next time bring Ellen for a free meal.'

You must be fucking joking, mate.

Okay Gerry I hear you…

I have found that the restaurant trade is a difficult one to make money in, even for those who are well experienced. it's hard work and you really need to be on your game. Many chefs enjoy cooking, but shy away from the commercial stuff, marketing selling etc., so they fail to get enough people through the door.

Most successful restaurants I have worked with are owner managed- they have skin in the game. This is a plus for Jon. However he has no experience in the business and listening to him, he is about to make the same expensive mistakes that others have made.

Jon has another issue. The location is out in the wilds, so he needs good reasons for people to beat a path to his door.

Several clients who have made money, decide to invest it in a pub or restaurant, in one case 'to teach the locals about good food'. His pub went bust in six months.

Back to Jon. He did not take any notice of my suggestions not that he needs to do. When I have been able to help restaurateurs, we have worked collaboratively, one step at a time: hiring good people, sorting the marketing, gaining, and keeping customers, buying effectively etc.

Jon has a dream, but no idea how to deliver it. He might be successful, but it will take hard graft and the ability to recover from expensive mistakes.

Chapter Fifty-Six

Homeworking

I **have been a homeworker** by choice. I run my management consultancy, for twenty plus years from my home office 'Cowshed HQ', in my garden.

Here are some of the survival tips and techniques I have learned since working from home.

1. I get ready – shower, dress, eat breakfast – every morning, as if I were going out to work. Otherwise I might still be in my PJs at lunchtime.

2. I set myself a work goal for that day to give me a sense of achievement when I deliver it. It's my way of staying fresh and motivated.

3. My mind is most creative first thing in the morning so that is when I do the important and innovative stuff. Admin and routine calls can be dealt with later in the day.

4. I like loud music in my home office, particularly if I am concentrating – Dire Straits, usually.

5. I work at the same desk every day, never at a table in the main house – it keeps me business-minded.

6. I notice that, when I am really focussed and 'in the zone', time goes at a different, much faster pace: 'Wow! Is it that time already?'

7. Clients seem to like leaving their city offices to meet me at 'Cowshed HQ' out in the sticks.

8. I like the separation of home from office (which is in a separate building, an ancient cattle barn in the garden) ten yards away from my back door.

9. Last week I completely tidied up and decluttered my office. It is immaculate. It gave me a feeling of being in real control.

Like everything in life, there are a few potential downsides:

1. Nobody handy to bounce ideas off or to provide another perspective.

2. No instant feedback, positive or negative.

3. No social chat, comradeship or fun.

My solution is to keep up regular contact visiting clients or via phone, Facetime and Zoom. I like working from home. Billy no Mates!

Chapter Fifty-Seven
A dream comes true

I enjoyed meeting Sally Wray, a business entrepreneur and young mum. We first met at an event held by our support organisation, For Entrepreneurs Only, an organisation I am proud to have helped establish. Asked about her background, she said, 'I was climbing the walls bringing up my three young children – so I bought a tool hire business!'

I was keen to find out more.

Sally welcomes me into her 'Gohire' office. She is tall, with striking long auburn hair and a warm, broad smile. Over coffee, she tells me some more about herself.

'My dad was a Butlins Redcoat, so we travelled around quite a bit when I was young. Then my parents bought a pub in Hull. Having left school with a C and two D's at A level and having failed my first year at Leeds University (had a fabulous time, mind you!) I got a job at Burger King. Hard work, but great fun. I learnt a lot there, about customer service and how to standardise a business so it that runs efficiently.'

'Hang on. Do you mind?' I say, digging out my notebook and ballpoint.

'No, go ahead. Next, I got a job at Hull City Council in the Housing Benefits Department. It was boring. I hated it. I jumped at the chance to work in their legal department when they offered it and I was proud when they promoted me to paralegal officer, but it wasn't all it was cracked up to be. I stuck it out for ten years until I was offered the chance of voluntary redundancy. I grabbed it.'

'So what came next, Sally?' I ask.

'I was a bored housewife looking after three young kids!' She smiles. 'So I started looking around for ideas. I took on a temporary college job in 2012 as a learning mentor, which I enjoyed but it didn't pay well. I told my husband, 'We need to make some money so I'm going to buy a business. He nearly had a heart attack!'

'Poor fella,' I say, and we laugh.

'It took three years, in fact. We considered a few unsuitable options and then, in 2015, I spotted a business for sale, a plant and tool hire outfit called Hedon Hire.' She pauses to sip her coffee. 'The owner was keen to sell. When he met me, a woman who was totally new to the business, he must have thought all his Christmases had come at once. He tried to stitch me up over the price and the value of the existing stock, but I am a quick learner and a stubborn negotiator. I don't think he expected that, and I didn't buy it.

'Around that time another hire shop, came on the market, called Arnott Plant Hire. Suddenly everything fell into place. We re-mortgaged our house and I added my redundancy money to buy the business.'

She points to the wall behind her, at the framed photograph of her standing at the entrance to her new enterprise, smiling as she holds up a set of keys.

'On the first day we walked through that door as the new owners, the oldest worker said to me, "You'll never make a million here, love!" I thought to myself, oh yes, I will!

'However, there was a lot to do. The place was a tip. It was filthy, with rats everywhere and a grisly awful smell. It was a miserable time, but my husband was a rock. He was totally supportive of my new adventure. We had no money to pay wages or buy stock, so we used our private credit cards beyond their limits. Terrifying.'

'During these dark days, Sally, did you ever regret your decision to start a business?'

'Not for one minute. I enjoyed being in control of my own destiny…. and I couldn't afford to fail.' She looked me straight in the eye and laughed. 'A key customer stepped in to help with the offer of much better premises – too big for us, but I decided to sub-let some of the space to a guy who wanted to open a café.'

'You inherited three staff – what were they like?'

Sally grimaced. 'There were some attitude problems. They thought they could manipulate me and get away with murder. I guess it's a bit unusual to have a female boss in a generally male-dominated industry. I got rid of two of them straight away and kept the third. However, the best move was to hire a new guy, Phil, who is brilliant. He manages the business for me now. Sales are booming and we are making good profits.' She smiles again.

'That's good to hear. So what made you join our business support organisation, For Entrepreneurs Only?'

'It's run by successful entrepreneurs who are willing to help other entrepreneurs succeed. I love overseeing my own destiny, but it does get lonely at times when I'm bouncing around ideas. The business start-up programme was brilliant. I was assigned a mentor, one of the top entrepreneurs in the region. He has been an invaluable help. I learned so much and I'm now running the FEO start-up programme, to support more entrepreneurs. I really enjoy this new role.'

She pauses. 'I should say, David, that I found your book, Entrecode, really helpful. I'm inspired by stories of entrepreneurs who have been there and done it. I take it with me everywhere, it is my bible.'

'Thank you, Sally, that's nice of you to say.' I'm always embarrassed by compliments. I press on. 'So, looking back, what do you think most enabled you to become a successful entrepreneur?'

'I think my previous work experience really helped – dealing with customers at Burger King, the legal stuff at the council, tutoring students and having to pick up a failing business up by its bootstraps. I share my story on the business start-up programmes. I guess I am a driven and ambitious person who mad keen on success. Oh, and it helps to have an understanding husband as well.'

'You've achieved so much in such a short time. What's next for you? '

'To keep enjoying what I'm good at – and to make that million!

Sally is a genuine entrepreneur. She has the vision to run her own business. She had no experience, but she is open minded and keen to learn. She never gets stuck or upset and her positive attitude helps her find a way forward. Her experiences have helped overcome her naivety, particularly when people are trying to take advantage.

I really like Sally. She is modest yet driven, juggling being a wife, mother and entrepreneur.

I'm sure she will achieve her dream.

Entrecode: Unlocking the entrepreneurial DNA, Management Books 2000 Ltd.

Chapter Fifty-Eight
Memo to my younger self

As I pass my seventieth year, I am reflecting on my life thus far. If I was to live it again, based on what I have learned, what would I do differently? Here are my reflections, in no order of priority.

1. Do not take your health for granted.

When I was young, I thought my good health would last forever. I was fit in my teens and played lots of sport.

Three decades later, when I was focussed on building my own business and working seven days a week, my wise sixty-five year old friend Raymond Elderton told me, 'You'll not be able to keep this up forever, especially when the aches and pains start to kick in and you are popping pills to survive.'

'Nonsense, Raymond,' I said, 'I'll still be still flying when I'm your age, mate!'

I was already overweight by then, a secret eater, living on a diet of junk food and not getting any exercise. By the time I'd reached my sixties I had developed Type 2 diabetes. Since then I have been unfit and overweight. I've tried every diet going but can't stick to them.

I want to be fit again. The support of experts has helped me improve other parts of my life, so perhaps it's time to hire a diet and fitness coach.

Wish I'd done it sooner.

2. You are not your job

I recognise I have been very one dimensional. Work has always been my priority at the expense of family, social life and most other things. It cost me my first marriage as I was often away from home, either working or studying, and paying little attention to my family.

Barbara, my first wife, told me, 'You are over-developed from the neck upwards, always working, studying and being away from our family.'

She was right. My children from my first marriage – Simon, Darren and Natalie – grew up largely without me and, although I try hard nowadays to connect with them and love them dearly, there will always be a distance between us I feel can never close.

At seventy I could retire – but to do what? Maybe that's my next challenge: to find a new purpose. Meanwhile, I want to be a better husband and father, whatever else I do. I really love my family and think I need to demonstrate it more. Writing this memoir has helped to reinforce that priority.

3. Value friendship

I have been fortunate to have had several close friends over the years, but fear that I haven't made enough effort in keeping in touch with them. At seventy, I now very much regret that.

A few weeks ago my brother Neville called me. 'David, I have some bad news. Jonny Mohan died while you were away. All the lads were at his funeral and asked after you.'

Shit. Shit! Hadn't seen Jonny for years. When we were teenagers, he was part of our gang. Together we set up a football team with no funds and went on to win the York League – real comrades in adversity. I felt sick in my stomach with regret and I do even now, as I write this. It was a wake up call and I have since made efforts to get back in touch with lost friends.

4. Decide in haste, repent at leisure

'We don't have longer term life plan so it's difficult to make short term choices. We should follow the advice you give to your clients and agree a life plan.' Wise words, as usual, from Ellen, my wife.

So now we are working on a long-term plan about what we want to do whilst we still can; a kind of bucket list of all the things we ever wanted to do but never quite got around to them. We are now in the process of prioritising filling the diary. As one wise person told me, 'An objective without a plan is a dream.'

5. Find a mentor

Throughout my life I have been helped by many people. Ray Elderton guided me in my career choice. Terry Bramall allowed me to experiment with his business like a laboratory, for thirty-five years, enabling me to develop my consulting skills. Gerry Egan taught me his brilliant strategy models, which I have used ever since to the benefit of many clients. These kind people helped me at important times in my life and I value them hugely.

However, for thirty seven years my most helpful mentor has been my wife. I have benefitted greatly from Ellen's wise counsel and support – and the occasional kick up the backside.

6. Be more adventurous

In many aspects of my life I have always been cautious, avoiding what I perceived as risks: I've travelled to safe places and avoided building relationships with new people. Ellen is much more adventurous than me, so I drive her crazy.

On a recent holiday to Sicily I made a real effort to strike up conversations with people and consequently got chatting to three interesting characters. I enjoyed it. I must work at being more adventurous because, as my friend Gerry Egan once said,

'This is not a rehearsal: this is it!'

7. Plan more to stay out of trouble

Years ago, my boss Hugh McCredie told me, 'There are two sorts of people, David: those that are good at staying out of trouble and those who are good at getting out of trouble. You are definitely the latter!' By trouble he meant the unwanted consequences of not planning in detail.

Getting out of trouble is always the more stressful option, so bloody well plan better.

But would my younger self have taken this advice? Probably not.

Chapter Fifty-Nine

Lessons from successful entrepreneurs

I **wrote Telling Tales to** share some of the lessons I learnt from the successful business I have worked with to help others.

So is there a pattern of behaviour in the successful entrepreneurial leaders?

If you have read this memoir then you will probably have probably be able to figure it out.

Here is my take on it:

1. They develop a long-term strategy based on their core strengths and their customers' requirements which provides focus and direction for everybody in the business. All the key decisions made are based on delivering the strategy.

2. They work ON the business and challenge and adapt it to the changing world.

3. They ensure they have the 'right people on the bus doing the right things'. They hire people who share their values but complement their skills.

4. They treat everybody, customers, colleagues and investors with

dignity and respect. This is a non-negotiable rule.

5. They have a clear set of values which they personally champion to make sure they get a culture by design, one they want, not one by default, one they don't want.

6. They 'let go to grow', delegating to colleagues to enable them to fulfil their own role.

7. They have a commercial mindset, understanding where the opportunities are to both make and lose money.

8. They engage in profitable partnering with customers and suppliers.

9. They try to maintain their entrepreneurial approach if possible. Often inquisitive, they learn from their life experiences, the environment, conversations and bring it back to their business. They recognise the dangers of becoming a stale, bureaucratic corporate.

10. They communicate with their people frequently and inspire them to go that extra mile, particularly when times are tough. They make rational decisions based on good management information.

Can these lessons be learned by others?

Well here is the good news. I worked with most of the businesses in this book. The majority used the Toolkits and with a bit of help revitalised or reinvented their businesses.

If you read their tales and use the Toolkits, you too can enjoy similar success.

Good luck.

TOOLKITS

How to get the best out of the Toolkits

These Toolkits were devised whilst helping entrepreneurs to develop their businesses over 40 years.

I watched and learned how they did their work and captured their wisdom and these Toolkits are a result of these insights.

Most entrepreneurs prefer to get their learning from other entrepreneurs, who have been there and done it.

It's often lonely being an entrepreneur, when I started my business in 1982, I looked around for help and discovered there was not a lot available that I found helpful. I devised these Toolkits to try to fill that void.

They have been used by many entrepreneurs in the UK, Australia, New Zealand, South Africa and Croatia.

Here is how to get the best out of them:

1. They are a guide; they are not a magic formula for success.

2. Read the memoirs and see how others have used them.

3. They are designed as a linear process, follow the steps and don't skip or shortcut any.

4. Engage colleagues in your business to help you.

5. They require you to work ON the business as opposed to IN it.

6. Success comes to those who take the process seriously.

Toolkit 1

Working ON the Business

❖ Significantly improve the performance of your business

❖ Use the wisdom within your business to develop it

❖ Introduce 'Best in World' practices to transform your business

This toolkit is very useful because it is a generic one that can be used in conjunction with several of the other toolkits to add real value to your business. It helps you to make significant improvements by harnessing the wisdom and energies of your people, empowering them to work **ON** as well as **IN** your business.

Often Managers are usually so busy working **IN** the business – solving problems and putting out fires – that they feel unable to spend the time working **ON** the business to improve it. Consequently, performance stays the same or deteriorates. The good news is that this toolkit enables you to address that problem and really improve your business performance.

Here's how to work **ON** your business:

STEP 1

Select your team carefully. Pick 3-4 people who are up for the challenge. Explain that you are going to work as a team to revitalise/ build/ improve/ change (pick your own phrase) the business and that they are all invited to participate.

Suggested criteria for the team selection. Every individual must:

- be keen and want to prove themselves
- be intelligent and motivated – they understand the proposition
- be someone you want to invest in for the future
- have a track record of 'delivery'
- have a cross section of experience and disciplines
- never complain they are too busy

Tell them you are not calling in experts or consultants. You believe that, amongst them, there is enough wisdom to improve the business. You will operate as a team to achieve that goal. This initial meeting could take 2 hours.

STEP 2

Agree on and establish the ground rules for operating as an effective team.

Typical ground rules:

- treat each other with respect
- no finger pointing
- be honest
- take the actions you agree to
- get the facts – no guesswork
- adopt a positive can-do attitude
- make it fun and exciting – an adventure, not a trauma
- be open to learning from best practice.

TIP: Ensure that the team contribute to the establishment of the ground rules so that they feel a sense of ownership towards them.

STEP 3

Sometimes the goal is clear, such as cutting costs by 10% or improving sales by 20%. The challenge is, how can we do it? Other times, there is a generic issue to address, e.g. to improve efficiency, boost profits or develop customer service. These kinds of challenge call for more analysis and investigation to provide a clear focus.

Get the team involved in the analysis of the issue/problem/ opportunity so that they really understand it. When there is a need for further research or investigations, encourage this process. The principle purpose is to get the facts.

Key questions to ask:

- What do we want?
- What are we missing?
- What is the real issue here?
- What would success look like?
- If we could solve one problem, what would it be?
- If it were my business, what would I focus upon?
- Can we do something that really adds value to our business?

Agree the issue(s) to be addressed.

STEP 4

Get new perspectives on the issue. A good way to inspire improvements in business is to ask, 'who does this best in the world?' Go and learn from best practice and see how it could be incorporated into your business.

TIP: Most insights come from reviewing best practice from outside your own industry because benchmarking against your industry has got you to where you are today.

STEP 5

Conduct trial and error pilots. Once a new opportunity or solution has been identified it is helpful to try it out in a low cost, low risk way. Does it work? If it does not, try something else. What lessons can be learned? Can it be scaled up? If the pilot works, the answer is yes. Now invest in it.

STEP 6

Celebrate and reward success and learn the lessons.

INSIGHT: Many organisations miss out from not introducing the benefits and lessons across the business. This is a major missed opportunity for many businesses.

SUMMARY

Working ON the business can create significant business improvements. It also develops your people's capabilities and confidence and creates pride in their performance and their contribution to the business.

Toolkit 2

Step Change

* ❖ Transform your business's performance
* ❖ Develop your key people
* ❖ Build the capability of your business to secure new opportunities

Over one hundred of my clients have made a Step Change in their business's performance over the past twenty years. The process has evolved by working with and learning from them. Here are some of their comments:

> 'Step Change completely transformed our business and set us up to grow way beyond our expectations.'
> **Martin Lauer, Owner, The One Point**

> 'Step Change transformed the profitability of my business forever. It's a simple process to follow and if you do, it produces results.'
> **Mark Eggleston, Owner, WJ Components**

> 'We put all our Branch Directors (53) through Step change twice from 2013 to 2018 it helped to increase our sales and profits significantly and it developed our managers capabilities.'
> **David Kilburn, Owner MKM Building Supplies**

Here is how to benefit from the Step Change process.

STEP 1

Learn from other entrepreneurs' experiences of making a step change

- Very few have a clear 3-year strategy to guide them
- Too dependent on the Leader
- Few work ON the business – too busy working IN it
- Some try to diversify away from problems which only makes things worse
- Many don't exit poor performers quickly enough
- Don't get the right people on the step change team

STEP 2

How to get the best out of the process

- Lead by example. Facilitate all the review meetings – shows your taking it seriously.
- Follow the process, don't skip parts
- 'Let go to grow' delegate to colleagues
- Keep pace in the process
- Insist that team members take the actions they commit to.
- Encourage colleagues to challenge the, 'we always did it this way' mindset.
- Encourage brutal honesty in the assessment of the business
- Get the facts -no guesswork or spin

STEP 3

Getting the right people on the step change team, is critical. Here is the ideal profile:

- Driven and ambitious
- Track record of delivering projects successfully
- Never claims to be 'too busy'
- Good at solving problems
- Good people skills
- Understands your culture but not inhibited by it.
- Maybe a younger person that you want to keep and develop.

STEP 4

Determine the 3 key issues to be addressed to make a step change in your business. Typically they include:

- Making changes to key personnel – Get the right people on the bus and the wrong people off it.
- Improving profitable sales.
- Cutting costs to improve margins
- Developing new products.
- Improving customer service.
- Installing more effective control systems and processes.

Select the three issues that will add most value to your business.

STEP 5

Crack on.

Appoint a team member as the leader of each issue to

be addressed. Make sure they understand they have the responsibility and accountability for their project.

- Communicate clearly to all in the business what's going on and why.
- Remove any barriers to progress – maybe back fill part of their role to enable them to have the time to focus on their project. Normally people spend a day a week on it to start, but this normally increases as the project develops and starts to get tasty.
- Encourage the project leaders to utilise other resources in the business to get the job done, e.g. other colleagues with specialist skills or systems.
- Ensure your people get the facts on the issue they are tackling so they really understand it and what needs to be done.
- Encourage people to look outside at other businesses who are 'Best in the World' at what you are working on. This can be both inspirational and provide valuable lessons to incorporate into your business.
- Meet regularly to review progress, with you chairing, say once a week to start with. Show enthusiasm and encourage people.
- Celebrate successes publicly and learn any lessons.

If you have followed these steps you should achieve the success you have earned.

Toolkit 3

Crafting Culture

❖ Design a culture that serves your business

❖ Develop consistency in 'the way we do things here'

❖ Make your culture an asset rather than a liability

Culture is best described as *'just the way we do things here'*. And *'what our colleagues do when nobody is looking'*.

Culture is your brand. How your business behaves, and the impression you create in the world.

If it serves the business, it can be a major **asset**. If it creates the wrong image it probably is a **liability**.

One client said, 'If accountants were smarter, they would put our culture on our balance sheet as it's our major asset.' This toolkit has been designed to help you to design and develop a culture, which really does serve your business. But first let's get to grips with what culture is all about.

Culture is:

- **A set of shared beliefs** about how we should do business – e.g. we believe we must deliver on time whatever it takes.

- **A set of values**, which should not be compromised – e.g. delighting our customers.

This creates **consistent shared behaviours** in the business:

- E.g., everybody from the receptionist, the drivers and the MD sets out to delight customers. This is non-negotiable and becomes 'just the way we do things here'.

Here is how to create a preferred culture.

STEP 1

Get your team together and establish your preferred culture.

Get them to brainstorm your core values. This helps get buy in to your culture.

You only really need six or seven core values, which describe how you want to do business internally and externally and which are critical to the success of your business.

Typical values:

- Delight our customers
- On time every time
- Treat each other with respect
- Being ethical in all we do
- Teamworking
- Collaborate rather than compete

STEP 2

Communicate and promote your values internally.

Talk with your people about your values at every opportunity.

TIP: Make sure you personally behave in line with the values.

Include the values in your key documents i.e., strategy, business plans, presentations to key stakeholders etc.

Explain what the values mean using live examples from your business.

Examples:

'We value putting our customers first. This means everybody pulls out all the stops to serve customers. In order to do that we will man the sales desk from 8.00 am through till 6.00 pm rather than 9.00 am – 5.00 pm.'

'We will agree and monitor service standards with our customers.

'Top managers will visit our key customers monthly.'

TIP: Values need to be translated into action by taking positive steps to live the values to make them drive business behaviour. People become cynical about values when they don't see the organisation doing anything to live up to them.

STEP 3

Get the culture owned in the business.

This means cascading the values throughout the business by allowing departments and teams to determine what the values mean for them.

Ask colleagues to decide themselves as a team what the **IN** behaviours and the **OUT** behaviours are for each value.

E.g., say the Value is: *Keep our Promises.*

IN Behaviours	OUT Behaviours
Act with integrity	Being negative
JFDI!	Being 'too busy to bother'
Now's good	Being average
Under-promise over-deliver	Over-promise under-deliver

STEP 4

Build your new culture into your business.

- Build it into your induction
- Review individuals and teams against it
- Hand out reminder cards to everybody
- Put up posters with the values around your building
- Talk about it regularly in meetings
- Get teams to audit each other on keeping to the values

TIP: It takes at least 18 months to install or change a culture.

STEP 5

Identify any blockages to the implementation of the new culture.

Working with your team, seek to identify any blockages in developing your preferred culture. These will probably include:

- **Covert norms** from the old culture i.e., 'We *always did it this way ...*'

or

'We *traditionally promote people using the civil service principle of length of service not performance ...*'

Covert norms need challenging and changing by establishing new rules, routines, and agreements.

- **Internal politics**

  Game playing between departments or individuals.

  E.g., *'Sales don't really talk to production they actually hate each other...'*

  or

  'Profit Centre Managers think HQ is a waste of money, so they do their own thing and ignore Head Office initiatives.'

  The politics of self-interest which are not in line with the new value need challenging and banishing.

- **Key holdouts**

  These are the people who refuse to imbibe the new values. They are wedded to the old ways of doing things.

  You really need to work on these people to get them to change. If they cannot and they are a major problem or threat to the business, you need to decide if one individual is bigger than, or more important than your business.

  In practice removing blockages to cultural change is often one of the most difficult tasks managers face in businesses today. Stick at it; the prize is worth it.

STEP 6

Set up culture review processes. This means ensuring there are rewards for implementing the new values and consequences for ignoring them.

And what happens to those dinosaurs who are unwilling to change?

Finally, integrate the new values into your existing processes:

- Make them part of the induction process.
- Include them in your business plans.
- Review the use of the values in your performance management system or appraisal process.

Toolkit 4

Cut Costs & Increase Profits

* Easiest way to make money is to stop losing it
* Cut out unnecessary costs
* Raise your own cash internally for investment

This toolkit has been used by many businesses to cut cost and increase profits. You can achieve similar success if you follow the ideas in this toolkit.

'We reduced our marketing spend from £400k to £40k and increased its effectiveness by using this toolkit.'
Simon Keates, North Staffs Caravans

'We discovered an additional £250k in profits that were hidden in our business.'
Paul Mackie, CEO, Rex Proctor & Partners

'We increased sales by 20% in 2012-13, plus another 25% in 2014. Profitability increased by 300% in 2012-13.'
Mark Eggleston, MD, WJ Components Ltd

The first principle in improving profits is to stop losing it!

This Toolkit is not a Step by Step approach. It is a series of actions to take that have produced good results. Choose the ones that suit your business:

ACTION 1

Consider putting your prices up

Too many businesses think they need to compete on price. Why? It is much smarter and more profitable to compete on anything but price unless your costs are much lower than your competitors. Consider using any of the following to get customers to pay more:

- Customer service:
  Go the extra mile and seek to delight and surprise your customers with the service level you provide.

- Product quality:
  Ensure your product is best in class in your sector.

- Personal relationships:
  People generally buy from people they like and trust, so develop your customer relationships.

- Delivery on time:
  Make sure you keep your delivery promises.

The principle is if you give your customers something worth paying for, they will pay you for it.

ACTION 2

Sell additional products and services to existing customers

When you have repeat customers, they buy from you because they trust you so they may be open to buying additional products/services from you. What else could you sell them? This is much easier and cheaper than trying to create new customers.

Our research shows that the best time to cross-sell more to customers is when they give you the first order not necessarily when you have been dealing with you for a while. So, be bold and offer new customers additional products when they first buy from you.

TIP: Check out how your customers use your products in their business and see if there is anything else you can provide to help sort any of their problems.

ACTION 3

Review your products/services profitability

Generally 20% of products produce 80% of your profits. Do you know which of your products produce your profits?

TIP: Analyse where you are making and losing money on your products and refocus on the profitable products. If you cannot do it find somebody who can, e.g. your accountant or somebody who is good with numbers. Consider dropping products that lose money.

ACTION 4

Produce a zero-based budget

Most businesses estimate sales then add up their costs and what's left are is profit or loss e.g.

Sales	£1m
Costs	£980k
Profit	£20k

The zero-based budget approach does it differently, e.g.

Estimate sales   £1m

Determine profit required   £100k

Therefore you can afford to spend £900k on costs. This then forces you to decide what costs are a must and what others you should cut. It is a very disciplined approach to boosting profits. It's also brutal, so make sure you are cutting non-essential costs.

ACTION 5

Negotiate, negotiate, negotiate!

When buying anything get into the habit of negotiating. Ask for a discount, extended payment terms or volume rebates. Seek to reduce your costs by 10% at least. Adopt the approach that there is no such thing as a *fixed cost* everything should be considered as an opportunity to reduce costs.

TIP: Read *Everything is Negotiable* by Gavin Kennedy. It's got great practical advice that many clients have found helpful.

ACTION 6

Inspect, don't expect

Don't assume anything about how people who work for you or with you operate. Check for any system slippage where individuals do not follow the process or rules you have established.

It may be your money disappearing out of the window...

TIP: Go and spend time with your people and see how they operate i.e. invoicing, credit control, costing, buying; nothing should be off your radar. Inspect, don't expect! If you smell a rat investigate!

SUMMARY

The easiest way to make money is to stop losing it.

Have a go at these six proven approaches and cut your costs and liberate your hidden profits.

When you do it well you will build up your own treasure chest for investment in your business. This is much cheaper and less risky than borrowing money from banks or other investors.

Toolkit 5

Delighting Customers

❖ Increase customer loyalty, get new customers from referrals and reduce price sensitivity

❖ Build competitive advantage

❖ Grow your business profitability

Delighting customers means doing the unexpected for your customers to create customer satisfaction beyond the norm.

If it is done well it can lead to high levels of repeat business, new opportunities coming from referrals from delighted customers and a lowering of sensitivity to price.

Delighting customers is more than just good customer service. Making it easy to do business, being treated with respect and getting queries answered does not delight customers, this is basic customer service. It's a right not a delight.

Delighting customers has the following additional qualities over basic customer service:

- Often spontaneous or unexpected.
- Delivered with a breath-taking speed of response, e.g. 'I asked about opening an account and they did it for me in less than 1 minute!'
- Outstanding attention to detail.

The benefits of delighting customers

- High levels of repeat business.
- New business from referrals from delighted customers.
- Lowering of sensitivity to price.

Most sane entrepreneurs would take these benefits.

The ingredients of customer delight

- Beyond their expectations
- Spontaneous
- A personal touch
- Speed of response
- Attention to detail
- Makes them feel important
- Puts a smile on their face
- Warm and friendly
- Different from the norm

How to create customer delight in your business

STEP 1

Ensure your basic customer service system is operating effectively (see Customer Service toolkit). You will not delight customers unless your basic customer service system is sound and consistent.

TIP: Check for any sales prevention officers in your business and keep them away from your customers.

STEP 2

Get your team together and explain that you want to build your business by delighting your customers. (See also *Toolkit 1: Working ON the Business*)

Brainstorm opportunities to delight your customers from the initial point of contact with them right through the business transaction until they pay the bill.

Use the ingredients checklist to help people recognise delighting opportunities.

Use the customer delight example checklist to provide ideas and inspiration to your team.

Checklist of ideas for delighting customers:

- Always seek to 'Do the right thing' with customers.
- Personally greet them when they enter the premises.
- Smile!
- Treat them like a best friend.
- Introduce them personally to your team.
- Give them your undivided attention.
- Focus on the details.
- Tell them about current special offers that might interest them
- Find out what interests them and talk about it.
- Solve a problem for them.
- Hire people who are good with customers.

STEP 3

Help stimulate your team's creative thinking about customer delight by getting them to talk with and learn from those businesses that really do delight customers. For example:

- Visit any Four Seasons Hotel anywhere in the world and see how they delight customers.
- Take them to a really good restaurant as a team to see how they delight customers.
- Find out in your area who delights customers well and arrange for your team to visit them.

STEP 4

Collect all their ideas on a flipchart. Decide which is only good customer service and which is likely to delight your customers. Agree the process and make it mandatory for all – non-negotiable.

Agree the customer delight standards. Get everyone to agree to delight customers and set up a system to ensure customers are constantly delighted.

TIP: Ask customers how they found your service and feedback the delight examples back to your team to reinforce the process.

TIP: Put delighting customers onto your meeting agendas and constantly seek new ideas to keep it fresh.

STEP 5

Conduct regular customer feedback sessions to establish how consistently you are delighting customers. Feedback the results with a sincere 'well done' to everyone. Fix any slippages or problems.

Toolkit 6

Getting Customer Service Right

❖   Create sustainable competitive advantage

❖   Keep your customers for life

❖   Deliver consistently good customer service

It **is well established** that customers are five times more likely to leave because your customer service is lousy, than because your products are poor.

This astonishing fact puts responsibility on businesses to get their customer service in shape.

What is good customer service?

It is the way you are treated as a customer from the first point of contact right through and even after you have paid your bill.

To check out your current service levels try to honestly answer these 10 questions marking yourself between 1-10:

It is easy for our customers to place an order with us 24 hours a day	1	2	3	4	5	6	7	8	9	10
We have a customer service promise that is kept	1	2	3	4	5	6	7	8	9	10
We give a friendly and professional approach to doing business with our customers	1	2	3	4	5	6	7	8	9	10
We interact well with our customers both face to face, over the telephone or on the internet	1	2	3	4	5	6	7	8	9	10
We have a consistent service offering irrespective of what time it is	1	2	3	4	5	6	7	8	9	10
We deal with all enquiries promptly	1	2	3	4	5	6	7	8	9	10
We keep customers informed on the progress of an order	1	2	3	4	5	6	7	8	9	10
Complaints are professionally and speedily dealt with	1	2	3	4	5	6	7	8	9	10
We have an excellent after sales contact program	1	2	3	4	5	6	7	8	9	10
We receive unsolicited letters of praise from over 5% of our customers	1	2	3	4	5	6	7	8	9	10

If you can honestly answer very positively (8 or above) to all these questions, then you have already got your customer service right and you are now ready to delight your customers.

However, many businesses in my experience will be doing well to answer three or four of these questions positively at 10.

We seem to have a problem in the UK with customer service. With a few notable exceptions, service is generally poor, which is why 67% of customers quit and go to competitors.

This is your opportunity, because if you can get your service right then this might be the way for you to gain competitive advantage.

Here's how to do it.

STEP 1

Start with your customers.

- Stand in their shoes and try to clearly understand what is important in terms of customer service.
- Visit them and ask what service standards they expect from you.

Tip: Consider doing a customer perception survey to discover what your customers **really** want and how well you are serving them. Be prepared for some surprises but that's why you are doing it.

STEP 2

Start measuring the service indicators established in step 1 on a monthly (or whatever period suits your business) basis. This is your baseline. Things can only get better from here ...

Some typical service indicators

- Guaranteed lead times
- Deliveries on time
- Technical support
- 24 hours back up
- Effective complaint handling
- Waiting times

STEP 3

Review your customer service through your customers' eyes.

Walk slowly and very carefully step by step, through your customer service process, from first point of contact through to paying the bill. Review the process in detail.

TIP: Get somebody from outside your business to 'mystery shop' your business and give you feedback. The brief is 'How good is our customer service?'

STEP 4

Establish service standards for your six key customer interactions.

The critical factor in getting customer service right is establishing a consistent approach to your customers. They don't want surprises.

Here's how to do it:

1. Establish your six key customer interactions. Ask your team for help. Use the checklist for reference.

    Checklist – Typical key customer service interactions:

    *   Providing a quotation
    *   Taking a message for absent colleagues
    *   Placing an order
    *   Asking for a price
    *   Chasing progress on orders
    *   Dealing with complaints
    *   Requesting information
    *   Checking availability
    *   Arranging meetings

2. Establish a small team of your people to produce a one-page step by step process of your businesses way of dealing with the interactions. Make sure you have

customer interfacing people involved who will have to use the process.

This one page should be bullet points and simple to understand.

This is your preferred way of doing business. The benefits of this approach are:

- It creates consistency
- The people who use it design it, which creates ownership
- The one-page process forms the basis for induction, training, culture building and monitoring.

3. Issue the new process to everyone concerned. Provide training in the process including inducting new people. Set up a simple monitoring system to check it works.

STEP 5

Get your management teams together and discuss, agree and take actions to improve your service levels.

One of the key issues in customer service is that it is not usually one person's responsibility. Many people can have their fingerprints on the process. Customer Service cuts across departments, as one MD said, 'Everybody is responsible for it but in practice nobody is responsible for it.'

This is the primary reason why it proves difficult to get customer service right. Therefore it is critical to get the real commitment of the departments in your business, which can affect your service levels.

- Review your internal customer service process.
- Consider mapping your internal customer service process to identify if there are any blockages internally.

Here's how to sort out internal customer service:

1. Get department heads together and ask them to write down what they want from their internal supplier (the department before them in the internal chain) and what they think their internal customer (next in the chain) want from them.

   One entrepreneur said, 'We have more competition internally than we do with our competition externally!'.

   Then get them to exchange this information with each other. They will be amazed how they are making life difficult (often inadvertently, occasionally with malice) for each other. This is called the 'silo syndrome'.

   Get them to agree to some internal service standards and communications and insist they stick to them.

   Review progress and ensure the internal service standards are adhered to.

2. Be prepared to have to make some significant changes to your business structure and process to improve your service levels.

Example

I asked the bank First Direct how they won all the awards for service on the telephone. They said, 'We hire nice people and nice people are nice to people. Oh and we give them intensive training for seven weeks before we let them near a customer.'

Make sure you employ people in the frontline who have good attitudes towards customers. Hugh Rice Jewellers hires for attitude and train for skill.

TIP: Make sure you don't hire any *sales prevention officers* in the customer contact roles. You can't afford them upsetting your customers.

How to perfect your customer service:

Here is a checklist based on the latest behavioural science research on customer service. Use it with your team to perfect your service.

- Finish strong. it's not first impressions that count, it's the last impressions. The end of the service is far more important because it's what remains in your customers' recollections. Cruise liners' trips end with dinner at the Captain's table. So how can you finish on a high?

- Get bad experiences out of the way early. Give the bad news early don't delay it until the end.

- Build commitment through choice. Let customers have a choice of at least two service options; this gives them perceived ownership and control.

- Give your customers rituals and stick to them, e.g. set up a weekly contact call and stick to it. Rituals build trust and confidence in your service.

STEP 6

Continue to monitor and review your key service indicators and take action.

- Your indicators should be showing improvements if you have diligently taken the appropriate actions.

  If they are not, then plan to take some different actions.

- Be prepared to train frontline staff in providing good customer service.

STEP 7

Communicate customer service improvements to all staff.

- Celebrate success, create heroes, and hold award ceremonies.

Toolkit 7

Intrapreneurship: Reinventing Your Business

❖ Unleash your intrapreneurial talent

❖ Create new opportunities

❖ Build exciting new business

Many businesses are now facing the need to reinvent themselves to survive. A way to do this is to unleash the entrepreneurial talent and energy you have within your business. In difficult times entrepreneurs create new opportunities often from practically nothing. Let's see how you can do it in your business.

Many of the traditional approaches to creating an internal entrepreneurial, innovative culture have not produced the desired results.

What has been learned about creating an entrepreneurial innovative culture internally, in an existing business might be called INTRAPRENEURIAL.

HOW NOT TO CREATE AN INTRAPRENEURIAL CULTURE

- Set up a 'special projects' team of 'volunteers'.
- Insist on measurable outcomes or objectives.

- Meet monthly.
- Appoint people to the team who have the time to be there.
- Insist on regular detailed reports and updates.
- Establish detailed screening criteria for new ideas.
- Throw money at the problem.
- Encourage the innovation team to be different i.e., dress down Wednesday mornings and all-day Friday.
- Innovate behind closed doors; keep customers in the dark in case your competitors discover what you are doing.

Many of the attempts to encourage intrepreneurship may have faltered because they contravene the ways intrapreneurs work.

Therefore it might be helpful to summarise the latest findings about how entrepreneurs do their work, i.e., the fundamental laws of entrepreneurship and then try to apply these lessons internally to create INTRAPRENEURSHIP.

1. *Entrepreneurship is now generally defined as* 'creating value often from *practically nothing*'. It is a resource-light activity, so throwing money at it may well be counter-productive.

2. Entrepreneurship is a creative act requiring vision, passion and obsessive commitment. It is mainly a right brain creative, intuitive process, so setting up committees insisting on detailed reports do not add value to the creative entrepreneurial process. In fact they inhibit it.

3. Entrepreneurs rarely have all the resources to take up opportunities and it is this tension between opportunity and lack of resources, which creates the energy to make it work.

4. Inventors are obsessed with their ideas. Entrepreneurs turn ideas into a product, which solve customers' problems and in doing so create a valued business Entrepreneurship is a customer-focused activity, so involve customers right from the start of the process.

5. Entrepreneurs develop their recipe for success by synthesising information from whatever source is appropriate or they personally deem credible.

If you compare some of the traditional ways of trying to encourage intrepreneurship by large organisations with the fundamental laws of entrepreneurship, it is not difficult to see why many attempts at intrepreneuring have failed.

If you need any more convincing, consider these two facts:

- 95% of all the innovations in the last 100 years, in radical new products and services, have come from businesses employing less than 20 people. Source: D. Birch, EfER Conference, Berlin, 1991.

- 50% of all fast growth businesses are run by people who worked for large companies, got disillusioned by the corporate culture, left and set up their own business. Source: John Case, The Origins of Entrepreneurship, Inc. June 1989.

- So don't let them leave your business; harness their energies in your business.

Enough of the theory lets crack on with helping you to unleash your intrapreneurial talent within your business.

STEP 1

Start thinking and acting as an intrapreneur.

- Talk to entrepreneurs to discover some of their attitudes, beliefs, and qualities. Read my book *Entrecode*, to understand how entrepreneurs create successful businesses.

STEP 2

Find and support the intrapreneurs in your business.

- Intrapreneurship requires vision, passion, and obsessive commitment, so find the people who have these qualities in your business and put them to work helping you transform your business.

- Ask people with ideas to come forward from whatever level or department. Give them the opportunity to pursue their ideas in your business – rather than 50% of them leaving to start their own business – at your expense!

- Listen to new voices. Younger people, new hires, etc.

STEP 3

Make it easy for people to start a business in your business.

- Give people space to experiment and try out their ideas. E.g., 3M allow all employees up to 15% of their time to work on their own ideas in the company's time.

  If the idea looks promising, they can spend a day a week on it, then if it gets even more promising, they can spend all week in the new incubator. If the idea takes off the company share the equity with the employee.

STEP 4

Bring Silicon Valley into your business.

Silicon Valley venture capitalists see an average of 3,000 new business ideas and plans per year. How many do you usually get? Well you can change that.

Silicon Valley works because it is a free market for:

- **Talent** – they don't care if you went to a top university.

- **Ideas** – they value good ideas from wherever they come.

- **Capital** – they try to make it easy for people to get capital.

How can you create Silicon Valley in your business?

STEP 5

Don't put bureaucratic blockages, even inadvertently, in the way of your fledgling intrapreneurs. Do not make the mistakes of many corporates; 'how not to create internal entrepreneurs.'

- Take any blockages out of their way that may be dissipating energy and passion.

STEP 6

Be prepared for some failures.

- If you are being intrapreneurial then you must expect some ideas to fail.

  You will be smart enough to ensure you do not bet your business on a bad idea too easily.

  As one MD said, 'If we don't get a few "no shows" then we are not taking enough risks.'

STEP 7

Encourage persistence.

- Innovation takes time, so encourage people to keep

going. E.g., it took James Dyson 587 goes to perfect his world breaking Dyson Cleaner.

STEP 8

Keep the process informal.

* Do not try to formalise the innovation process, allow it to germinate and grow. Intrapreneurship is an informal, often trial and error, process. You need to try to keep this informal for as long as possible.

Toolkit 8

Lessons from Entrepreneurial Leaders

* ❖ Think and behave like an entrepreneur
* ❖ Develop the capability of your people and your business
* ❖ Provide Leadership

Is there a pattern in the beliefs and behaviours in successful entrepreneurial leaders? If you have read this memoir you may have been able to work, it out. Here is my take on it.

An insight for me from writing these memoirs is that the most successful entrepreneurs I have worked with over forty years, live by many of these beliefs and behaviours.

Good leaders understand what their people want, and this guides their behaviours:

* *Behaving with Integrity is a non- negotiable.*
* *Communicate openly with me.*
* *Do what you say you will.*

Here is how to behave like a successful entrepreneurial leader:

STEP 1

Adopt the **personal beliefs and behaviours** of successful leaders:

- Driven to succeed – possibly the key behaviour.
- Resilient and persistent, using setbacks as rocket fuel to crack on.
- Learn by doing and from the best people.
- Low on ego, high on humility
- Treat people with dignity and respect
- Commercial mindset – know where to make and lose money.
- They communicate in a way that really inspires their people.
- Key mantras that guide their behaviour:
  - KISS -keep it simple stupid!
  - Keep the eyes on the prize
  - Communicate. Communicate. Communicate.
  - JFDI!

STEP 2

Colleagues

- Invest in developing colleagues.
- Provide coaching to enable colleagues to achieve their career aspirations.
- Practice 'tough love' to help colleagues deliverer outstanding results.
- Ensure Colleagues share in the success they help create.

STEP 3

Customers

- Use customer perception surveys to identify opportunities to build competitive advantage
- Identify customers problems, solve them, sell the solutions to the world
- Seek to delight customers. See *Toolkit 5: Delighting Customers.*
- Establish long term mutually beneficial partnerships
- Create new products based on trial and error experiments
- Make it easy for customers to do business with us.

STEP 4

Revitalising the Business

- Let go to Grow – see *Toolkit 9*
- Unleash entrepreneurs within to improve profits and cash flow – see *Toolkit 7: Intrapreneurship – Reinventing Your Business*
- Apply insights from 'Best in World'
- Rethink the traditional business model – disrupt the industry
- How well do you do comparing yourself to successful entrepreneurial leaders?
- Hopefully, the stories and Toolkits in this book will help you.

Toolkit 9
Let go to Grow

* ❖   Delegate successfully to grow your business and yourself
* ❖   Create a team-managed business
* ❖   Identify and remove any major obstacles to growth

One of the biggest challenges faced by growing businesses is to successfully empower a team-managed business. This innovation allows the leader to focus externally, on longer-term issues, rather than the day-to-day performance of the business.

Many clients had found the limited capacity of their management teams was the biggest internal barrier to growth.

Why? There could be several constraints on those individuals responsible for the business:

* many demands on their time and energy
* the need to work on several things at once
* being consumed by the day to day but at the same time worrying about the future.

From personal experience, many of the traditional business remedies to these problems tend to be half-hearted, with little constructive follow-up.

These don't really work:

- attending a time management course
- attending a team building workshop
- trying to 'delegate' to people, but reluctantly

When top managers try to 'let go', they find it too difficult to relinquish control, constantly interfering and annoying people, or they abdicate completely. Neither approach is effective. This toolkit will help you to be smarter than that.

Here's how to do it:

This is a time-tested way of dealing with the emotional issue of letting go, delegating and sleeping easy in your bed.

STEP 1

Clarify your own role in the business for the future. What should be your priorities?

Try using the **prioritising method** i.e., our strategy/plans/priorities call for .... therefore I should be focusing upon ....

If you are the leader then your key leadership tasks include:

- setting the strategy
- picking capable people to deliver the strategy
- spending more time building the business for the future, perhaps as much as 50% outside the business, interacting with customers and stakeholders
- encouraging working ON your business (See Toolkit *Working ON the Business*)

STEP 2

Once you have decided your role, consider what aspects of your role you intend to delegate to others and then decide:

- who is capable and ready for development?

- who has enough energy, commitment and enterprise to relish the challenge?

TIP: Try picking some young people. You don't have to be 64 to manage projects or companies!

STEP 3

Tell these carefully selected people that you intend to focus on some key areas and therefore intend to personally delegate part of your role to them. Emphasise your belief that they are ready to take on a bigger role and give them the responsibility and accountability to undertake new tasks.

- Agree the objectives with them in detail (the 'WHAT')

Examples:

'Objective: to look after and improve the distribution of our products and increase the "on time" delivery performance from 65 to 95% over the next six months.'

'Objective: to launch three new products by the end of 2020 as part of our agreed business development process.'

STEP 4

Ask everyone to produce a one-page action plan outlining the steps they intend to take to achieve the objectives (the 'HOW').

- This plan (a mental rehearsal) allows them to do the thinking, develops their confidence and gives them ownership of the task.

- It also allows you to check their thinking and plans, before taking any action.

- You can either sign off the plan or coach them in any areas for improvement. Either way, they own the task, the job gets done – and you sleep easier in your bed.

STEP 5

Make sure you are available if required but offer your advice if requested.

- This is particularly important when you are moving from an owner-managed to a team-managed business.

- Remember: you know how to do things; you have probably spent years working at it

- The tasks may well be new to your people, so you must invest time in passing on your experience. So delegate and coach don't abdicate and hope...

TIP: Don't fall into the bureaucratic trap of trying to record everything you do in a system manual. You need to build the business by building your culture (see *Toolkit 3: Crafting Culture*).

STEP 6

Continue to show interest in their work. Continue to use their action plans to assess progress. Congratulate them publicly on their successes.

STEP 7

Focus on your new role without falling into the trap of either getting over- involved in the delegated task or abdicating from it, only to worry about what is happening.

TIP: Learn to master the three Ds: Do it, Diary it, or Dump it. You will create time for the important tasks you need to complete.

SUMMARY

If you 'let go' effectively, then you will create more time to focus on the important aspects of your role.

288

Toolkit 10
Redoing Your Strategy to Revitalise Your Business

❖ Create a new future for your business

❖ Focus on your business strengths (internally) and market opportunities (externally)

❖ Improve your businesses performance

Very often businesses get locked into an existing strategy and then find it hard to change, even though world is changing fast. One way of revitalising your business is to review and refine your current strategy.

But first what is *strategy*?

- Writing a long doc?
- Thinking 'outside the box'?
- Working harder?
- Something the directors do.

I have reviewed most of the models and information on strategy and concluded it's none of the above. After 40 years helping clients design and implement strategies, I believe it is:

> A set of actions designed to overcome the biggest
> hurdle(s) in achieving your long-term objective.

Let's break it down:

- *the objective*: needs to be clear and shared by everybody in the business.
- *set of actions*: there needs to be a concrete plan.
- *overcome the biggest hurdle(s)*: needs to be a clear diagnosis of the hurdle(s) and the plan should focus resources on overcoming the hurdle(s).

Here are the 3 key steps in designing and implementing a successful strategy.

STEP 1

Strategy Design

Strategy is usually designed by a small team led by the business leader addressing the following questions:

Q. 1 What business are we really in?

This question is answered by addressing questions such as:

- What opportunities are there in our markets?
- What do our customers want?
- What are we good at and where do we make money?
- What should we stop doing?
- What's our competitive advantage?

The idea is to focus on market niches, which are growing, profitable, and where you have the skills to serve them effectively.

When you are reviewing your strategy, *the difficult part is not doing more but less*. Cutting out loss makers, and nostalgic products which may be consuming valuable resources. The aim is to prioritise around 3 or 4 key market choices and the same number of products/ services.

Q. 2 What will success look like in 3 years' time?

Once you are clear about your business focus the next decision is: 'What will success look like in the future?'

- The best way to address this to ask 'If we were celebrating our success in say 3 years' time what would we have accomplished?'
- You need to ensure there is something compelling for your customers, colleagues and investors.
- If you want to take people with you on your journey you need to have something for them that inspires them and keeps them engaged.
- This vision does not have to be a repeat of the past, it is usually aspirational.
- Also do not worry how you will achieve it, that comes later.

Q. 3 How do we want to behave and compete to deliver your strategy?

- Your brand is much more than your logo, website or marketing materials. It's how you behave and are perceived by the world.
- Your image should be deigned rather than leaving it to chance, people will judge your business, good or bad -whether you like it or not.

- The way to do it is to agree your 5 or 6 key business values. E.g. Delighting customers. Behaving with integrity, etc
- This process creates your culture.

STEP 2

Identifying and overcoming the biggest hurdles to be solved

Now comes the hard bit. Implementing your strategy.

The way to start is to conduct a SWOT analysis, Strengths. Weaknesses, Opportunities, Threats against your new strategy. Most people are familiar with this approach.

In implementing our strategy what are our SWOTs?

You may develop a long list, but the next step is to prioritise the key hurdles you need to overcome to deliver your objective?

I have found it's best to consider the 3 main hurdles in year 1- you can't deal with 17 priorities.

Typically the hurdles are:

- Getting the right people into the key positions, doing the right things. Inevitably this can mean moving some people in or out of the business.
- Getting costs under better control.
- Improving the sales and marketing system.
- Developing your digital approach.
- Etc.

You need a plan for overcoming each hurdle, allocating responsibility to individuals for each one. Ask them to produce their plan with timescales, resource requirements and reporting arrangements. You can then sign off their plans.

You now need to ensure everybody prioritises the plans and cut out any distractions.

STEP 3

Communicating your strategy

- Engage everybody; colleagues, customers, suppliers and investors in understanding and helping to deliver your plans.
- Hold briefing sessions with everybody to explain the strategy, and importantly encourage and answer any questions.
- Some clients have distributed cards to everybody summarizing the strategy. Others have put up posters around the workplace.
- Bring the strategy to life and explain to all what the benefits could be to them personally.
- The plans should be reviewed regularly(monthly) but not at a normal board meeting when current short- term business issues inevitably take priority.